JOURNEY TO THE MIDDLE OF THE FOREST

A Maryland Half-Life

Bruce Fleming

Hamilton Books
A member of
The Rowman & Littlefield Publishing Group
Lanham · Boulder · New York · Toronto · Plymouth, UK

Hamilton Books
4501 Forbes Boulevard
Suite 200
Lanham, Maryland 20706
Hamilton Books Acquisitions Department (301) 459-3366

Estover Road
Plymouth PL6 7PY
United Kingdom

Library of Congress Control Number: 2007936262
ISBN-13: 978-0-7618-3893-7 (paperback : alk. paper)
ISBN-10: 0-7618-3893-7 (paperback : alk. paper)

Part of Chapter Four originally appeared, in another form,
in the Sewanee Review. Part of Chapter Seven, in another form,
originally appeared in the Southwest Review.

Table of Contents

Preface

Most of the memoirs that sell are written by famous people: they're the backstage to the public drama, and the simple folk like us are interested in them for that reason. We feel a delicious *frisson* at seeing that public personae have private sides too: here's what she looks like without her makeup! Here's what he really likes to watch on TV! Some memoirs are more high-toned: who but a serious intellectual would be interested in the memoirs of, for example, James Merrill? Still, it's a back-story: you have to like Merrill's poems to be interested in the memoir.

A small number of literary memoirs stand on their own, as witnesses to their time—perhaps Edmund Goss's *Father and Son* is of this sort. And J.K. Ackerley's *My Father and Myself* may have its enduring charm as a result of the arch way in which he tells the story of his father's double life and two families, the contrast of off-hand narrative style with the events he narrates.

Perhaps Victorian memoirs are doomed to be about the Father, that overarching *pater familias* in the waistcoat with the frown and the pocket watch who controlled people and things to the grave, and sometimes beyond: even Virginia Woolf had a go at him in her memoir of growing up at "22 Hyde Park Gate." He was the great bug-bear of childhood that had to be slain by the adult memoirist, his authority debunked as mere show—as all children-grown-up-to-be-adults realize it is. But we're no longer Victorians. We're also no longer Modernists, or even post-Modernists. What's left to debunk? A memoir that will endure past the first breathless "I can't believe that was Elvis's favorite sandwich," must nowadays be about something more abstract than a person. Such as, I suggest, the belief that life has an intrinsic structure.

Most of the time we're content to live in the shadow of those deemed worthy of our attention: political figures, entertainers, sports figures—and the products they use and endorse. We follow and discuss their issues, their games, and their shows. So long as we fail to reflect that what we "have" to have this week, the people we "have" to know, the restaurant we "have" to go to, aren't the things we "had" to have last week—so long as we're content to revel in the sheer transience on it all—we're fine. But if it's so transient, why should we be so interested in it? It's when we start to reflect that what seems solid really isn't that we begin to despair. Is there no permanence to the world? No objectivity? If our sense of solidity comes from taking for granted the Interesting and Important, what do we do when we realize that we collectively create the illusion of Interesting and Important?

Virginia Woolf, in her story/essay "The Mark on the Wall," spends pages reflecting on the fact that she doesn't know something—what the mark she sees on the wall might be—and that even if she did, it wouldn't matter. The objective (which for Woolf meant: male-determined) world would tell her she was being ridiculous. This world would say: Get up and find out what it is! Invest your time and energy in something more than a mark on the wall! But would the world be justified in saying this?

Woolf reflects that people before the Great War certainly thought the difference between Importance and Unimportance absolute, as shown by the "Table of Precedency" in Whitaker's Almanac. You could look it up: who preceded whom into dinner, lined up in numbered order, from the King down to a provincial administrator—it was in the middle that things got dicey. Yet by the time Woolf was writing, all this had crumbled: people laughed at the notion of this false absoluteness, the notion of objective Importance. Let them go into dinner as they please! Even the most absolute of objective structures can simply go away. And what do we make of that?

The messy reality of our lives—our childhood, our marriages and divorces, our children so different than we'd expected—diverges not just from this illusion of absolute Importance, but also from the channeled, polished, simplified things we typically present to others. And that's something the new memoir can, and should make clear: what it's providing the "back story" for isn't Father, or even Celebrity, but the way we package ourselves for others. Inside, we're not a bit like that.

This contrast is clearer to me than to many people, because I've lived for twenty years in the spit-and-polish "you can do it!"/"look good for outsiders" world of the U.S. Naval Academy, where I teach English. Appearance at the Naval Academy is, to a large degree, reality, as is "motivation." Mere effort, people are told, suffices to accomplish your objectives. Our students, midshipmen and future officers in the U.S. Navy and Marine Corps, are told that they can accomplish anything they want if only they try, and that "showing up early and looking great" are the two most important things they'll need to do. Their parades, which the tourists thrive on—row upon row of identical trim bodies in perfect rows, moving in unison—give outsiders a taste of sunny perfection, whatever growly thoughts they might be thinking as they stand in rigid formation. The point is to cut the grass and the hair, inspect the uniforms, and revel in the illusion of predictability and order it affords—not to consider, say, the world of the beetles underfoot (a world that Virginia Woolf was for that reason quite interested in), or the disorder that these rifles, could they actually be fired, would inflict on the world, or the inaudible things the midshipmen are saying under their breath to the commands (for "pass in review" they say "piss in your shoe"). And as for achieving anything you set your mind to: by the time they realize it isn't that way, they're gone from the Naval Academy, and usually from the Navy as well. Besides, this is the military, that famously takes individuals and throws them in handfuls against a foe: where's the self-determination in that?

It's all beautiful at Annapolis, the order and the belief that individuals control their destinies. But that's the point: it's an illusion, a created effect. All perfection is. That doesn't mean it's illegitimate, only that it's a façade. We can prop it up if we choose, create our own Potemkin villages. But at least we should know we're doing it.

The point of a literary memoir nowadays must be to show the messy reality of a life and its contrast to the order we project to others. There's nothing wrong with projecting it: others love basking in the illusion, which is why we project it. However problems arise when others confuse this lovely illusion with reality. As a result of contacting only people projecting their public personae, many people make the mistake of thinking that they alone lack such order. In fact, everybody does. The illusion of order is, first of all, an illusion. It's only achievable after the fact: we wait for the dust to settle after the crash, and then appear, saying "*voilà*! That's what was supposed to happen!" And it's made for others' consumption: we never sense it while we're in the heat of living. It's not illegitimate, this illusion, but it does carry a price tag, require sacrifices. This memoir, a "journey to the middle of the forest," tries to remind us of the price, the sacrifices we make to get the illusion of order. The greatest of these is, a denial of the reality of what it feels to actually live life. Memoirs of the rich and famous, for starters, get this one completely wrong: their lives in fact feel to them as ours do to us. Their apparent greater interest is in the eyes of the beholder, not of the person inside the life.

We don't share this publicly. My emotionally stunted father, my brother's death from AIDS, the great dreams of my first marriage that all came to such an ignominious end, my bi-polar step-daughter who helped put an end to the marriage, my learning-disabled daughter: all this is replaced by the façade of a hearty handshake, a three-piece suit, and a smile. Yet it doesn't go away. We make things up as we go along, and then try to pretend that that's the way they had to be. Because everyone else does the same thing, we end up feeling that we're the only one lacking solidity. This memoir, presided over by the Goddess of Uncertainty—as all of our lives are, could we only admit it—has as its intention, therefore, to provide comfort: we're not alone; everybody else is just like us. For a brief time, in reading it, we can all let fall the mask of structure, solidity, and inevitability we project to others. In fact, we're all in the middle of the forest, lost in the thicket of our own life. The best we can do is to say, looking back, how we got here—but not how to get out, nor even where out is. And now night is coming on.

Annapolis, Maryland
July 2007

One
EVEN CHICKENS ARE CHIC

Drivers and Passengers

When we read about other people, we don't want to find their lives beset by the same uncertainty that defines our own lives. We want, if not glamour (attainable by most of us normal people only if we pay enormous sums to stay in five-star hotels), then at least certainty, and a clear life trajectory—something we ourselves by definition lack. We also want to be told that life is worth it. Not may books will admit that the jury is still out on that one—that, despite early June days with cloudless skies, small furry animals, and transcendent performances of Schubert, life may simply too much heartache and disappointed hope to be borne; that it's a world, to quote Matthew Arnold from "Dover Beach," that "seems/ To lie before us like a land of dreams,/ So various, so beautiful, so new" yet "Hath really neither joy, nor love, nor light,/ Nor certitude, nor peace, nor help for pain."

This book makes this admission. It admits too that life is a voyage whose pattern can only be determined after the fact, and from the outside: a journey to the middle of the forest, from which we only emerge at death. Anything we do is part of our life: we're all like the clown from *I Pagliacci* whose death throes are thought part of his act.

Living our own life is like being the driver of a car along a winding road at nightfall, the wipers whipping against the increasing rain, the road now instinct, the darkness closing in. We grip the wheel, sit up, and stare at the road, and can hardly take the time to talk with the passengers. We're focused on staying on the road and not going over the side of the mountain or into the ditch. Our lives aren't over yet, and we remain steadfast in our belief that we can influence them: they're ours to change—at least, so it seems to us. Hearing about someone else's life, by contrast, is like being the passenger. The person next to us at the wheel is the one in charge. We can afford to enjoy the scenery, since there's nothing we can do anyway about where the car is going. So we can relax, sit back, and enjoy—as disembodied voices in airplanes, and now sometimes theaters, enjoin us to do.

Memoirists are drivers imagining themselves as passengers. As they tell their story, it seems to them they are hearing it from someone else other than themselves. And so their own lives seem more coherent than they would otherwise have done. This is so even in the case of a story told from the inside, like this one. I can say how I got here, but I can't say what it means, or where it's going. Still, it seems more solid than life as lived.

Eastern Shore

This particular journey to the middle of the forest is also the voyage to the middle of a century. It covers the years 1954 to, for round number purposes, 2004, when my father was still alive and my older son just born. I grew up in Salisbury, on the Eastern Shore—the Eastern Shore, that is, of the Chesapeake Bay, on the peninsula that is called Delmarva because it includes Delaware, some of Maryland, and a tiny sliver of Virginia. It wasn't until adulthood I realized this was the source of the name I had simply taken for granted, thinking it as inscrutable as the Indian names of Wicomico (the county) and Pocomoke (next good-sized town south).

In recent years, the Eastern Shore seems to have acquired something of the same cachet as a place to be from as, say, Newport—and something of the same associations. Enough Old Money has been able to hang on to palatial houses with columns and endless driveways with views of stagnant rivers, and enough well-to-do Washingtonians and New Yorkers have built summer homes in the central region of the Eastern Shore, around the town of Easton, that the whole region has taken on a the air of a playground for the rich and exclusive.

When I was growing up, however, the Eastern Shore was all flat sandy fields and chicken farms. Even the chickens have become chic in the meantime, with the televised whine of Salisbury native Frank Perdue heard during the 1990s in living rooms up the entire Eastern Seaboard, and the birds that are grown under franchise to him by dozens of farmers in the area (chickens which he somehow manages to sell on the grounds that they are full of fat) on sale in almost every Manhattan supermarket.

Since then the downside of the chicken industry has become apparent. An outbreak of a mysterious water-borne fish rot called pfisteria was traced to the dumping of chicken manure in the rivers. The processing plants (one of them is the first thing people who drive into Salisbury are aware of, and if the wind is right—or wrong—considerably before) are dangerous and bloody. A trade in illegal Mexican workers to man these plants has grown up all over the Eastern Shore; sealed trucks with the bodies of stifled immigrants are found more and more often along the trail into Salisbury and its environs. Quaint if down-at-the-heel towns of Anglo farmers suddenly have enormous sub-communities of Latinos, and the local Catholic churches run as many Masses in Spanish as in English.

In the 50s and 60s, however, all this was in the future. The Eastern Shore had yet to be discovered as the slower-paced oasis next door to Metropolis: back then it was just poor, flat, sandy, and covered with soybeans. It was only in 1952, the year my older brother Keith was born, that a permanent bridge was built over the Chesapeake Bay at Kent Island, which sticks out into the Bay and diminishes appreciably the distance between the shores. Before that the few people rash enough to make the trip had to rely on ferries. Many people on Delmarva, my mother assures me, opposed the bridge, seeing it as a means to allow an invasion by city folks. They, in turn, seemed to think that the bridge was rolled up in the winter. The beach-goers didn't need it then, did they?

Even now, there is animosity between the Eastern and Western Shores of the Chesapeake Bay. A comment by the bizarre and opinionated former mayor of Baltimore and sometime governor of Maryland, referring to the Eastern Shore as "the shit house on the other side of the Bay," made it to bumper stickers proudly displayed by its residents that assured anyone who cared to read it: "I'm from that shit house on the other side of the Bay."

Salisbury is the largest town on Maryland's portion of the Eastern Shore, boasting during my youth two high schools (three before segregation was ended, now once again three with population growth), a main downtown area decaying even then, in the pattern of American small towns that would see their business bled off to malls and these in turn abandoned for bigger malls, and a "colored" commercial section gone to seed after the early 1960s and the Civil Rights Act, right across the river from the formerly "whites only" shopping area.

There were many rural black people who picked produce in the fields; our beloved Amy, who helped raise my brother and me while my mother returned to teach, did so in the summers well into my adolescence. In terms of race relations, Salisbury during my childhood was considerably south of Mississippi—though the local storeowners had, in the 1960s, seen the writing on the wall and signed a non-discrimination pledge that saved Salisbury from the incendiary protests that rocked nearby Cambridge, somewhat slower to catch on to the dawning of a new age. A few miles outside this hub and everything is chicken farms and soybeans; further down toward the water, it is marsh grass, Victorian houses gone to ruin, and trailers.

People in Salisbury tended to be phlegmatic, to talk as if they had a mouthful of potatoes, and to think Salisbury the center of the universe. The movers and shakers came, with few exceptions, from Baltimore or Wilmington, and had settled there in search of a more peaceful life style. As a result the moving and shaking was kept to a minimum. My mother had come from even further afield, from Albany, New York, via NYU. She came because she was married to my father, a local boy.

We grew up in the shadow of education, my brother and I—what at the time was the State Teachers' College, STC (already a step up in development from its birth as a State Normal School), that in the 1960s mutated into Salisbury State College, SSC, and, decades later, into Salisbury State University, SSU. In its most recent and grandest avatar it has metamorphosed into "Salisbury University," as if hoping that people would think it was ancient seat of learning, and not merely a "state school." Both my parents taught at STC/SSC/SSU, my father in biology and then education, my mother in music. For a number of years, my mother was the senior faculty member: forty-some years in a place where she never felt at home.

The literary claim to fame of the college in Salisbury is that it serves as the setting, under a fictional name, for the novelist John Barth's first book, *The End of the Road.* Barth grew up in Cambridge and was briefly a student at Salisbury; his heyday was in the postmodern 70s, writing duly self-reflexive fiction that now seems merely grim in its relentless playfulness. The portrait of the college he offers is not flattering, but since there is no such thing as bad publicity, some years later they awarded him an honorary degree.

High school in this rotten, provincial small town was, of course, dreadful: my brother and I were too flip, too different—notorious, but certainly not popular, because vociferously anti-athletic. My high school years were the usual story of a sensitive adolescent, my high school quite typical for small-town high schools of no particular renown, my unhappiness there utterly banal. Or perhaps I'm getting the causality wrong: certainly my snide couch-potatoism, which lasted through college, was the result of the fact that so much emphasis was put in high school on the physical, and by people I didn't want to be like (or rather, and this the tragedy: people I did).

The world we perceive as children is fundamentally different in its structure than the world we perceive as adults. We see the objects and experiences of our childhood like stone monoliths erected by a civilization so powerful and so long gone that their leavings must simply be navigated around, taken for granted, accepted as fact. Unable to conceive of alternatives, we accept as givens this teacher, these fellow-students, these desks with these scratches, this scraggly patch of trees in this backyard, this set of parents, this particular road of joy or humiliation.

At the same time, all of us have within us sights and sounds that have bonded to our beings during that period when things seemed foreordained, when the world truly was our world, rather than merely a place in which we lived. Childhood is beautiful in retrospect precisely because we seem, at the time, to have been trains rooted to the track stretching before us: our worlds are given, and we at home in them, without possibility of alteration. And then with adulthood we come to understand that all is contingent, our own lives included, and the contingent never tastes the same to us as the absolute world of our childhood.

Yet growing up is not, as Wordsworth apparently thought, merely a loss, an ever-increasing distance from the nirvana of childhood whose clouds of glory dissipate as we move ever more inexorably into the prison-house of adulthood. Growing up can be a great liberation from the particular. Because children lack the ability to see things in relative or abstract terms, they are prisoners, held captive by the givens of their world. Freedom is found only in the ability to achieve abstraction, because we can define our needs and set out to find the things that will fulfill them. Children have no such freedom. Developing it is necessary for life itself, but doing so means giving up the absoluteness of childhood, which we never regain.

Everything in my situation conspired to render me an outsider, to deny me the belief we so long for in childhood—and that so constrains us as adults—that the way things were was the way they had to be. Thus I achieved this freedom earlier than most people, or rather had it thrust upon me: the particulars which fuse to our eyeballs as the only possible world were forcibly ripped from my eyes.

I know something that I think most people have to work hard to discover: what is, is contingent. It can alter. Perhaps not today, and not tomorrow. But someday, somehow, sometime. The mere fact that "everyone else" tells us this is the way things must be means merely that $1 + 1 + 1 + 1$ of people in the world don't see it our way. And what does it matter that this list of one-plus-ones is very long? It's still just one-plus-ones, an accretion of people who, individually, are no more important than we are.

Pygmalion

Both my parents were alienated from their surroundings, though for different reasons and in different ways. My mother was a geographical outsider: she had come from the city to the insular, agrarian, and sleepy Eastern Shore. She then found herself stuck in a bad marriage with a man more different from herself than she could have imagined.

My father grew up some thirty miles down the road from Salisbury, near Pocomoke, and should, at least for this reason, have been at home. However, he too was an outsider in his own fashion. My father interacted with the world by belittling it, my mother insists, in order to protect himself from rejection. He criticized his students for being stupid, his wife for having her own life, and his children for being unwilling to accept his views as gospel.

My father believed strongly in quantifiable intelligence. No one was as intelligent as he. Or practically nobody; on this one issue he accepted his sons as allies rather than rivals, making it clear to Keith and me that we were far more intelligent than anyone around us. On this one issue too he was gracious in defeat. I remember him telling me at an early age that he had learned from our elementary school principal, a colleague of his since our elementary school was the demonstration school of the college, that my IQ was higher than his own. He said this with the rueful admiration of someone acknowledging himself fairly bested.

For her part, my mother the music professor never failed to make it clear that this place we had been born into was utterly bereft of culture. Furthermore, she had grown up thinking art galleries were interesting places, and dance something worth looking at. The Eastern Shore had none of these things. From junior high on, therefore, we piled into the car every other Saturday for the two and a half hour trip to Washington, where these things could be found. First we would go to my violin lesson, then to Keith's cello lesson, then sometimes to Keith's orthodontist appointment, and then usually add on an afternoon in the National Gallery or a matinee by the now-defunct National Ballet of Washington. We'd eat our lunches out of the lunchboxes shaped like school buses that were too useful to throw away but too childlike to use in public. And then we'd go home again, having passed the day in this so-different world. Now it's my world.

By my mother's standards, and hence by Keith's and mine, the people on the Eastern Shore talked funny. If we heard once we heard a hundred times: "I don't want you to grow up to talk like an Eastern Shoreman." People there talk about spending a "quudder," drinking "wudder," build with "see-ment" and take out "in-shuhr'nce." "Hey budddey," the Eastern Shoreman asks, "ya wanna go over't the bahr t' geyut us a burh?" The conductor of the College Choir for many years, my mother gave us repeated lectures on enunciation: as a child, I remember giggling on her cue about how her students always wanted to sing about the "Virgin and chahl" in the Christmas carols, which of course was inevitably followed by the "mother mahl." Pronounce ending consonants, I learned.

Like Shaw's Eliza Doolittle therefore, I am a constructed speaker, the gender-flipped Galatea of my mother' s Pygmalion—except of course that there, the metaphor falls apart completely. We are all the creations of our parents, who love us, but differently and less possessively—with any luck—than the sculptor loved his creation. The real point of the Pygmalion and Galatea story, it seems to me, is the artist's alienation from real women and his self-absorption, not his professed love for his creation. That part is silly; we never love, romantically love, the things whose workings we too well understand because we have created them ourselves. Writers don't love their own books, though during the process of writing them they seem more important than life itself.

I speak the way I do because of a great deal of concerted effort. Because my mother continued to work full-time even when Keith and I were small, she had help in the form of Amy, who cleaned, cooked, and served as our second mother. She encouraged Amy to take the summer farm jobs early on because, by dint of being around her so much, Keith and I had begun speaking her idiom. One of the stages on the way to my educated coastal American English, with the consonants properly pronounced and no flattened vowels, was rural southern black speech.

My mother's sense of alienation from her surroundings even had its topographical expression. If I heard once, I heard a hundred times about the lack of hills on the Eastern Shore, flat as the proverbial pancake and covered with sand. "Oh, such beautiful mountains," she would exclaim as we headed north toward the Catskills from New York City those summers when we returned to Albany to visit her family. And on return to Salisbury she would sigh, "No mountains here," as if discovering this fact for the first time.

Now she has a house in the Adirondacks, which reminds her of her childhood. Besides, she likes mountains, as indeed I do myself, much preferring a mountain vacation to a seaside one. At the same time, however, I look inside myself and find the childhood (and hence irreversible) conviction, born of my mother's tutelage, that people who lived near mountains were smarter, better, and in all ways superior human beings to those who lived in the sandy flatland.

"How did I ever end up here?" my mother would ask with a rhetorical flourish. We knew the answer, so kept quiet. Still, she has now lived more than fifty years in this place without hills where she felt so alienated. Where else does she have to go? The shoes may chafe when new, but finally they adapt to our feet. Or is it simply that we lose the will to protest?

The worst time with my father was after dinner, when he demanded my mother sit at the cleared-up table, a dutiful wife keeping her husband company where he was most comfortable. He would read the newspaper aloud, punctuating articles about politicians and current events by sarcastic comments about the things he was reading, while she tried vainly to follow the thread of the book open before her. Again and again he would interrupt her to point out the idiocy of the world, until finally she gave up books and took up needlework, which, she told Keith and me, she could continue even in the midst of his constant interruptions.

My mother was better known in the community than my father, not to mention much better liked, because of her activities with the College Chorus. Handily enough, her salary even in those pre-feminist times was equal to his, so there was never any talk of her quitting her job and sitting around the house full time. On those rare evenings near holidays when, because of a rehearsal for an upcoming program, she came home late, he would be sitting waiting at the kitchen table, positively beside himself that she had not spent the evening there with him, doing nothing. He expressed his pique in needling comments to make clear to her the enormity of her offense. How they made her feel I'm sure he never thought, or perhaps did, and made them for precisely that reason: the comments scratched his itches.

Anything short of complete and utter subservience made my father red in the face, and sometimes caused him to scream and yell and throw things. My mother claims that when Keith and I were little, my father was a loving parent, taking us to the cooperative nursery school wearing his white lab coat. "When you got old enough to have your own opinions," she says, "all that changed."

The denial of the individual's right to be him- or herself: this is the greatest wrong a person can do another. Which, of course, is not to be confused with letting others do the things they most immediately want to do. Parents are set up by fate for getting this wrong. Many parents are so conditioned by the helplessness of their infants they think they can maintain the same attitude towards the child, the adolescent, and even the adult. Many men, especially, think of their children as nothing but extensions of themselves: in the argot of our time, men see themselves as "passing on their DNA." Yet any individual's DNA is only half-transmitted, and is itself only the momentary fleeting combination of many great-grandparents', like a kaleidoscope frozen arbitrarily in mid-turning. When it combines with a partner's—itself an amalgam of countless other people—it is thrown once again into the great vat from which we are all ladled out a spoon- or individual-full at a time. What is this belief that we can replicate ourselves?

Yet many men want their children, especially their sons, to be "just like them." Let's say they win the lottery: their son looks like a younger version of them, adores them, acts like them, and is equally successful in the same field. How great is the probability that their sons' sons will do the same for them? Or is that simply not the father's problem? Did the father who so wants to be perpetuated himself perpetuate his own father? It seems unlikely. Really what this strange desire to "pass on our DNA" means is that we ourselves deserve to be replicated, but do not have to replicate anyone else. But why do we deserve more to be replicated than others do? Not to mention that replication is utterly out of the question. We ourselves are just chance combinations produced by a certain sperm arriving first at the egg, a certain set of mutable events in our childhood, and the chance of the circumstances into which we were born.

Men too seem to think they control their offspring. Nothing could be further from the truth. This is so because of the intrinsic asymmetry of parenting: the parents regard their children as their creations. For the children, however, the parents are mere facts of life: they've always been there, and are givens like walls and tables. Children can be forced to revere their parents, but it isn't even clear this is a good thing: too great dependence leads to its own set of problems. In more recent years I came to see that my mother was just as relentless in her attempt to control as my father: what worked for children didn't work for adults. It all seemed peculiarly inhuman, as if neither of them could read cries of agony—I don't *like* this—as anything more than a challenge to be overmastered.

Stones

In my early 20's I decided that intellectually I was the offspring not of my biological parents, but of two "stones," my spiritual father the philosopher Ludwig Wittgenstein (Stein = stone in German), my spiritual mother the self-absorbed "If I think it's interesting you will too" writer Gertrude Stein. How odd that a young man raised in the 1950s on Maryland's Eastern Shore who likes women should feel akin to two long-dead European-based aesthetes, both of them homosexuals. This shows that transmission is never direct. Our children may be far more unlike us than someone who won't be born for another hundred years.

It would actually be reassuring if I could still feel towards my father the hatred I felt towards him with the passion of early youth. That would suggest that such things have real value, are in some way absolute. But the unnerving fact about life is that with distance, everything fades. My father was not a good father, any more than he was a good husband. My mother still hates him for the second. But I can't hate him any longer for the first. At this distance, my memories of him have burnt out, like leprosy running its course, becoming the pale, almost invisible outlines of their former selves, like scars almost having blended into my skin.

Of course, if prompted, I can call back the feeling of myself on the kitchen floor, my father's shoes kicking viciously into my side; I can recall the time when, at the dinner table, with the radio news blaring, I began talking and my father threatened to run me through with the steak knife he held with white knuckles, his face contorted in fury. I was acting counter to his will. He wanted to hear the news. But it is with a feeling no stronger than faint interest that I press these buttons: they seem like the sound of a radio heard from a far-off apartment in a building on a summer night, distinguishable from the other more immediate noises around it—the crickets, the sound of people laughing and talking—only as a result of intense concentration. The valence of things doesn't alter, they merely fade. This is what we can't tell the hot-headed young, who would merely find us shilly-shalliers, unfocused, and lacking in clarity.

My father was and is—though for many years he lived in an Assisted Living Facility where his actions are more circumscribed—an alcoholic. According to my mother, he would come home from work full of stories of who had said or done whichever stupid thing, and fill a big glass of bourbon and water. This would be about 4 in the afternoon. The glass would be repeatedly drained and repeatedly "sweetened" until he stumbled into bed at 11.

Certainly the alcohol must have killed its share of brain cells; I remember coming home from college to see my father, who always lorded his intelligence over those around him, being stumped by the plot of a Perry Mason re-run on the television. This seemed to me evidence of a major sea change. Indeed the mere fact of a television set, a recent acquisition at the time, seemed evidence of his intellectual decline. That we in our family did not own a television in the 1950s and 1960s when television was new had been one of the defining facts of my childhood. This had been so for all the right reasons: both parents educators, television a "boob tube." On this, as on many other issues, my parents were right. To be sure, it meant that I was bereft of normal subjects of conversation with my classmates, consisting largely of what had happened on what show the night before.

Now, as the father of a daughter with autism-spectrum learning disorders, I have acquired vocabulary that to a degree fits my father as well (this may be coincidence: such conditions aren't, so far as science knows, hereditary). People with Asperger's Syndrome, a label used to describe people like my daughter with a "ghosting" of autistic traits, have trouble understanding that other people exist. They are in an almost literal sense solipsists, the state of Descartes before he concluded he could at least be sure he existed: thinking that all those curiously shaped things walking about below his window were only machines, or figments of his imagination. "Aspies" can't empathize; their selfishness is so complete it seems self-evident to them.

I think my father was an Aspie before the fact. He lacked the ability to read the most basic social cue: he couldn't process agony as agony, disgust as disgust, humor as humor, disinclination as disinclination. Nor did he even interact with others: he merely decided the way things were going to be, and then resisted absolutely if others had any other view. There was no such thing as discussing with my father, no acknowledgment on his part that anyone else had a leg to stand on. Nobody but my father, in his view, took up room: everyone else merely got in his way.

Because of having grown up with my father, I know what others discover the hard way, or sometimes not at all: that other people typically can't be convinced of much. They're brick walls. Of course my father was extreme. Yet I remain convinced that there's not really much point in arguing with people: they are what they are, and words are unlikely to change that. Art is the one thing that is human but typically doesn't argue: it states its case and they walks away. It doesn't bang you over the head. Is this the reason I love it so much?

Terms such as this one of "Asperger's Syndrome," that I am tempted to apply to my father as well as my daughter, change the way we see things once they take on substantiality. People become examples of the general, rather than merely what they are. The French thinker Michel Foucault, insisting that scientific naming actually alters the world, would have a field day with contemporary psychology, which delights in diagnoses that for millennia didn't exist. The debate currently rages, for example, over whether what we call attention-deficit disorder, ADHD, is a real thing, or a taxonomic invention.

Foucault's point is that if we "have" X, as in "having" measles, where X is conceived of as an independently existing thing, we become merely the unimportant variable on an unchanging set of givens. We change, they stay stable. It denies in some fundamental way our individuality. This is the loss of accepting the "scientific viewpoint." Yet what we get in return is that this now-separated aspect of ourselves can be targeted independently: we can be cured, of it or at least we can seek a cure. If cancer is something we have rather than something we are, we can look for a way to make it go away. If we don't separate it out conceptually we can't conceive of it going away without taking us with it. Foucault is fundamentally a Romantic, nostalgic for a terminology that stops with the individual, even at the price of not being able to effect cures. If we as an individual aren't separate from our condition, the one science separates out as X, we can't be cured of it either. It's part of us, and we must take it for granted.

Because my father interacts socially with no one but me, he's an absolute individual. So there isn't much point in seeing how closely my father's case fits the paradigms of a medical diagnosis. It wouldn't change a thing. What we set out to know is a tiny subset of all the things we could know: we deal with the world on an as-needed basis.

Given my father's authoritarian view of human interaction, it's not surprising that the only part of his life that ever made him happy was his association with the Army. Such organizations give the illusion of absolute clarity to relationships, after all, something Aspies seek. I learned a number of years ago that the dream of his childhood had been to go to the U.S. Military Academy, West Point. Is it any wonder we have been reconciled completely by the fact that I teach at the U.S. Naval Academy, Annapolis?

He spent many years as an officer in the Army Reserve, which he entered out of college in 1934, and retired as a colonel. He filled the closets of the tiny house we lived in while I was in elementary school with his uniforms, and went every summer on active duty to places he sometimes took us with him to, like Fort Sill, Oklahoma (where my brother and I saw our first tarantulas legging their way across the path outside the off-base motel we lived in, and Geronimo's cell), and Fort Benning, Georgia, which had a wonderful Officers' Club pool where we went every afternoon (I have been more sunburned on army posts than on the entire rest of the Earth) and a library that by children's standards was excellent, where we spent the mornings. I remember cool inside rooms, and pages and pages of Tom Swift and the Hardy Boys, the delicious world of these so-badly-written books no adult should ever re-visit.

Money

Our childhood was, to the extent that my father was paying or influencing the purchases to any significant amount, tawdry and poor, full of faded old things and occasional cheap new ones. I remember countless "tourist homes" instead of motels, faded houses with creaky beds and mildew on the shower curtain where frumpy women in housecoats showed us to our room, countless McDonald's hamburgers, then I believe only 19 cents (the reason my father liked them), and innumerable versions of objects that broke, split, dissolved, or simply wore out after the first using. With two equal salaries in the family, even if only of State Teachers' College professors, we were solidly middle-class, and could have afforded the normal middle-class amenities. There were, however, battles over every nickel, things denied us with an explosion because they were "too expensive." I'm sure that anything we got, my mother simply bought for us, or had to fight for.

Though surrounded by the cheesiness of middle-class America—a tawdriness that also caught Nabokov's eye and made it to the page in *Lolita*— and the plastic cheapness of the few things my father bought for us, Keith and I were at the same time growing up amid luxury. My mother had inherited from the one wealthy member of her family, one of her father's sisters who had married political money in New York State, a vast amount of household furnishings from a more opulent era, along with all of her jewelry and furs. This was the time of Tammany; I'm not sure that Uncle George, whose ring I wear and with whose personal silver I occasionally still eat with, led a political career above reproach. Some time ago the fur coats dried out and had to be replaced, but my mother still wears Aunt Pauline's diamonds and gives parties with her two sets of silver; polishes her marble-topped French furniture, turns on her jade lamps to read, walks on her huge Persian rugs, and sits to read in the heavy overstuffed armchairs that defined the parameters of my childhood.

My father's immediate influence on me has been minimal since I was about 14. Yet when Keith and I were children, he was a tyrant who controlled our lives. I meditate on the contrast between the enraged Cyclops that dominated my formative years and the shuffling, grossly overweight old man in the tattered clothing (he won't buy anything new), who mutated into the pitiful old man after his stroke with a lot less fat. Once he bestrode my world, only to end as a barely visible dot on the far-off landscape. This should have been the riddle of the Sphinx: What is first overwhelming, then interesting, and finally unimportant and trivial, all without changing in the least? Answer: our parents.

I think too: people should be careful how they treat their children. All things being equal, children will live to see the parents grow old and lose their power. It will help at this point if the motor behind the relationship has been something other than coercion.

In the case of my brother, all things were not equal. It was my father who sat and watched my brother die, and not the reverse. For years before this, Keith would not speak to him. Their stand-off ended only when Keith became ill. Then, much to my surprise and contrary to all my expectations, my father (who learned simultaneously that Keith was gay and that he had AIDS) re-entered the family, coming every day to see Keith, paying the horrifying hospital bills that my insurance-less brother incurred, and uttering not one single, solitary word of reproach. How to explain that the tyrant, the Army Colonel, would accept so immediately a gay son dying of AIDS, and this without any apparent shred of gloating or "I told you so"? How to explain that the miser who had ruined our childhood with his obsession with pennies would write checks for tens of thousands of dollars without batting an eye? Was it regret? The attempt to buy love he knew he'd lost? Genuine lack of censure with respect to people he was no longer responsible for? I'll never know; I'll never bring it up with my father, who probably wouldn't have any idea what I was talking about if I did.

I take this to define a liberal: presupposing that all people are in principle amenable to communication. Alternately, we can make the presupposition, which I take to be emblematic of conservatives, that people are intrinsically the Other. Conservatives of course aren't hermits, so their exceptions to this general rule are defined in advance: those who are members of their families, or their nations are held to be Inside, all others Outside.

For conservatives, the line between these two absolute groups is clear from the get-go. For liberals, the line dividing inside and outside remain to be negotiated.

Liberals want to wait to see on a case by case basis whom they can talk with, and whom they have to shoot at. There's no absolute line. To conservatives, this means liberals think all the world is their friend. This, conservatives point out, is clearly not the case. But rejecting the notion of an absolute line doesn't mean there isn't a distinction; it's just one we have to determine. And on this issue, I think, liberals are clearly correct. Just as I can be more like a long-dead Austrian philosopher than my own father, so my father's being my father doesn't mean I can communicate with him. Conservatives will insist till they're blue in the face that things are simple: love the people Inside, who are like you; accept the difference of and be prepared to meet with force, the people Outside. Fine, but the fact is we don't know who falls on which side of the line.

I like to think that I am sufficiently removed from the level of the playing board that I understand the principle by which the pieces are moved, rather than merely being conscious of my own motion. But there are two people in my life whom I can never hope to see from such a distanced perspective: my ex-wife, and my father. I know from my contact with both that we can so strip the normal gears of interaction with another person that the only link left is one of civility: not politeness, which requires some greater acknowledgment of the person than I can now feel, but the mere unsmiling, monosyllabic answering of questions posed. Even recrimination, though negative, is at least a connection.

However, I did once try recrimination on my father: it was an attempt at check that he handily mated. One night, when my father was well into his 80s, he was spending the night at my house in Annapolis on his way back to Salisbury from a doctor's appointment at Walter Reed Hospital in Washington. I had spent all afternoon with him in enforced socializing. By dinnertime I was restive, perhaps a little unfocused. He had been drinking, as usual, and began to talk about the past. In his version, astonishingly, everything was fine, with a perfect family and him as the respected patriarch. I was silent, abruptly possessed by the feeling that if ever I was going to talk to him about this, the time was this moment. What the hell? So I allowed the floodgates to open: the violence, the arguments, the miserliness.

Then it was his turn. He didn't take it lying down. First he denied everything I had said, then he lashed out, countering with theories pickled in bourbon over long evenings of how my mother had purportedly been unfaithful to him with many men—including her childhood friend who was now a Catholic priest. I told him he was crazy and left the table. The next morning, he seemed to have forgotten all about the conversation. So much for reaching out.

My parents were divorced more than thirty years ago, when my mother decided that enough was finally enough and moved out. My father re-married a few years later, a lumpen country woman whose primary motivation, it finally became clear even to him, was his moderately comfortable amount of money. I think even she came to see that she had married the world's most self-centered man; they too were subsequently divorced. This brought the total of his wives to four.

In the penultimate act of his life, after his last divorce, my father spent his days in his lamentably dirty house watching videos from the public library and noting down his reactions (*The Blue Angel*: "didn't like"), planning his funeral, which was to be orchestrated by the local chapter of the Veterans of Foreign Wars, and going to the funerals of other VFW members: the VFW provided the van, and he took along a camping stool, as part of the mourners' claque. Here I cannot resist bending the convenience that constrains this memoir to an even half-century. My father died in 2005; by the time he did so, the VFW mourners' claque had itself been decimated by old age, and his graveside service, rather pitiful because attended by only a few sparse family members, was put on by, of all people, my mother. She must have felt at some level she had won the fight between them: she got to bury him. She had already gotten to bury my brother on her terms, which I think gave her a feeling of vindication as well.

The terms in which I conceptualized my father were, I now realize, largely those of my mother, who from an early age felt the understandable need to get some of her own back by talking about him to her children. Because she didn't view divorce as an option, making clear to her children that his way was not viable was the only way to stay sane. What a travesty their marriage was, how full of heartache on her part and sheer maliciousness on his. My mother cannot simply cut it from her life: there would be, relatively speaking, so little left over. We can reject something, but all that we reject is ourselves; in the same way that we are composed of the bodies of all those who came before us and nourish ourselves from the food grown from their compost. Perhaps I can learn something from this regarding my own travesty of a first marriage, that colossal blunder at the end of my emotional youth. Because it was her life, she is still fighting its battles. Our lives are apparently composed only of the blind ends of our mistakes. How can we separate them from ourselves? It's a good thing no one is giving us a grade on our lives; we'd all fail.

Thus I understand my mother's point of view, but can't adopt it. There is no one in the world to whom my father continues to mean as much as to my mother, albeit negatively. There's no one, therefore, who sees things the way my mother does. Similarly, no one but me knew Keith, and Keith is dead. Recently I read a heart-breaking letter to an advice columnist: the writer had boxes of carefully sorted family photographs, but no one to give them to. She was in despair: if nobody takes over your memories, what's the point of having them? The advice columnist, trying to be compassionate, suggested a local historical society. That at least was better than no one at all. And what if in the local historical society they simply grew dusty? Even memories passed on to people we know weaken to the point of irrelevance: for my children, the Uncle Keith who died before their birth is only a few photographs and a story or two. As we ourselves will one day be.

Incense

My mother had a theory to explain how she came to be linked with a man so different than she: when she met him in New York after the War, he was dashing and urbane, her professor at NYU, where he had gotten one doctorate and where he was teaching a course or two while working on another doctorate at Teachers' College, Columbia. My mother's perhaps too-neat view of my father is that, removed from the haunts of his dirt-poor childhood haunts, he briefly took on the polish of his urban surroundings: it was in this phase that she met him. And then, in her word, he "reverted." Reverted, that is, to his childhood on coming back to its haunts, as if the world my brother and I too grew up in had blighted, cast a pall over this man, their marriage, and thus our lives.

The wedding itself posed a problem, given that my mother was Catholic, and my father had been married twice before. His first wife was dead. She had been a hairdresser in Crisfield, Maryland, where he had gone after college to teach in the local high school. Crisfield during my young adulthood was a decaying cluster of houses and stores with peeling white paint on the edge of the Chesapeake Bay, best known, and that only locally, for the annual Blue Crab derby. There were crab races along great wooden troughs, and other things associated with country fairs. The festivities culminated in the crowning of a local beauty as Miss Crustacean. At least, to break my own rules again, that was true until the arrival of condos on the water in the later years of the twenty-first century's first decade, as part of the movement that led to urban waterview apartments taking over dying Chesapeake Bay hamlets on both sides of the Bay.

This first marriage was not, from the point of view of the Church, the problematic one. The glitch was the second, in New York, to a woman of aristocratic Hungarian background. I've seen her family's palace in Budapest. Erna, so I understand through my mother, who heard it from her sister-in-law, was an artist, teaching at the Pratt Institute.

After only a few months of marriage she, or perhaps both she and my father, realized that a mistake had been made. A civil annulment was therefore procured (to a civil marriage, though I suppose Erna, being Hungarian, was probably Catholic), on the trumped-up grounds that she had discovered after the marriage that her husband did not want children. In fact, it seems, neither of them did, but clearly this justification for annulment seemed more believable than any of the alternatives, which included imbecility of one partner and non-consummation. Though a prude who never talked about the body or its functions with Keith and me, my father was I believe, something of a sexual dynamo until an advanced age. I believe his physical attentions were utterly unwelcome by my mother, and wonder if this is one reason why she never remarried. (Her fury at having been controlled and manipulated for decades was surely the primary reason: never again.)

According to the Church, therefore, my father, a Methodist, was still married to this woman whom he had wed in a civil ceremony, and therefore not available for my Catholic mother to marry. She must have been independent even then, because, though she was devoted to her Church, she married him anyway, and was duly excommunicated.

My mother's own parents were themselves a Catholic/Protestant mix. Her mother's family was South German, which is to say, the Catholics, and my grandfather's family North German, the Lutherans. Her mother had raised her children as Catholic, as back then was required for such unions. Because of the excommunication, Keith and I were raised, to the extent that we were raised in a religious sense, as Methodists.

Of our religious education, there remain the memories of watery Kool-Aid during summer Bible School, an equally sugary picture of a beautiful man with flowing blond hair and beard emanating rays of light from his head, and earnest Sunday School teachers. I also remember my vigorous participation in a pageant held in the church basement with pipes running across the ceiling, where I played Saul/Paul in a bathrobe and got to cry out, "My God, why have you forsaken me?" Or perhaps this is not what I said, but something else; what comes back to me when I bite on that particular rotten tooth of memory is, at any rate, a sense of intense embarrassment, though I hardly know any longer for what. Perhaps the fact that as children we cannot see ourselves as we will see our childish selves once we are adults.

In Salisbury, my mother did not go to church. During the summer, however, when we went to visit her parents and brother's family—then later only her mother, then only her brother and his family—she did. These visits to Albany, which blur together into a whole that looms larger in my childhood memory than it must have been in fact, are punctuated by visits to incense-laden dark interiors, sonorously-intoned Latin—this was, of course, pre-Vatican II, when the language of the Mass was changed to English and many other signs of modernity were incorporated into Church practice—and the ringing of many bells.

My most lurid ecclesiastical memory is one Feast of Corpus Christi, High Mass in the church where my mother had gone as a child: little boys in white gloves, little girls strewing rose petals from baskets, the stench of incense, the portentous undulations of a language not so much understood as simply re-evoked vibrations of one's own body. Now, I am sure, I would remain unmoved: as a child, however, I was very affected. We always left the Mass just as the people began streaming up the aisles for Communion. Even in Albany, in a place where the officiating priest, probably himself only recently arrived, would have no way of telling her from any of the other parishioners, my mother stuck to the terms of her banishment.

Compared to the full-lit earnestness of Methodism, the tenebrous, incense-clouded rites of my mother's forbidden Church could not have seemed anything but exotic and alluring. I remember an adolescent religious experience or two which made me think I too had to become a Catholic; then Vatican II, as the Second Vatican Council is called, Protestantized the Church, and I got older.

Local boy

From New York, therefore, the young couple went to Salisbury, where my father had gotten a job where he wanted to be, fewer than thirty miles from his birthplace. Local boy makes good, that's how my mother saw his motivation: and armed as he was with an Ed.D. from Columbia and a Ph.D. from NYU, she is convinced that his plan was to become president of the college. The fact that he spent his time publicly criticizing everyone he came in contact with for their dull-wittedness and stupidity may, she notes, have played a role in the fact that he never achieved this goal.

Another major factor in this "reversion" in addition to the sheer weight of place was, in my mother's view, his mother. My grandmother was not a likable person. My mother referred to her mother-in-law when out of her hearing as "that dried-up old witch," though she continued to do necessary things for her until she died, far more diligently in fact than my father.

I remember my grandmother as a wrinkled old woman who lived in a little wooden house down the road from ours, in the settlement of Fruitland, outside of Salisbury. She spent her time sitting on the porch in a rocking chair, watching for cars and stray dogs and spying on the neighbors. "She was the most *negative* person I ever met," my mother still sometimes says with great emphasis. "Except Father," she adds, using the term we use to refer to him by between ourselves. To third parties, he is "The Colonel."

My grandmother seemed perennially worried that somebody would blame her for something; her laying blame for a broken vase on the then-toddler Keith (justifiably, it seemed) the instant my mother walked in the door after a baby-sitting stint is something that was replayed over and over in our household. "Keith did it!" my mother would screech, imitating her mother-in-law's shrillness. Not that my grandmother was wrong in thinking that she was frequently blamed: my father ordered her around so much that each time he left her house she was in tears. When I complained about him to her she merely scrunched up her face, flapped her hand, and said, "Don't notice it, child. Don't notice it."

During a period of several years until her marriage, my grandmother was a one-room schoolteacher in Somerset County, Maryland. Her teaching certificate hangs in my office, bearing a date more than a century ago, July 25th, 1901. The certificate itself, that is to say the empty form, was already more than twenty years old when it was filled out in spidery handwriting to attest to the capabilities of Miss Marion O. (for Olivia) Mills: the engraved date reads "Eighteen Hundred and Eighty___." This portion of the engraving has been crossed out in a single neatly-ruled red line skewering the center of the letters, and the numerical date from the new century has been written in the blank, in sepia ink. On another shelf behind me sits her school bell, as she herself had kept it as a remembrance of what may well have been a happier time.

July 25: my own birthday. It was also on another July 25, this one in 1941, that my grandfather, her husband, walked into the barn with his shotgun down in Westover down in Somerset County, where my father grew up, and shot himself. Family lore, unsubstantiated, suggests that he had Parkinson's disease and was unable to work any longer, or walk behind the mules with the plow. In his turn, my father has Parkinson's disease. Perhaps I am next in line, if the disease is inheritable; I am told that doctors are divided on this issue.

My father had one brother, two years younger than he, whose way through college my father paid. My uncle also went to Teachers' College, Columbia, where he got an M.Ed. When Eastern Shore folks got advanced degrees, it was in primary or secondary education, a glorified version of something all of them had been exposed to. They became teachers, or teachers of teachers, not professors. My uncle, in my father's version of things, resented him all his life for having helped him early on. "You should have left me down on the farm," my uncle is supposed to have told my father.

My uncle was wounded in a Normandy beach assault in WWII; my father made his war contribution as an instructor of something, in Rome, which may be why he continues to think so highly of the military. As a result of his combat service, my uncle had physical problems all his life. When he lay dying years later of three or four incredibly painful conditions, my father wrote him a letter that he, my father, proudly quoted to me, telling his brother that he had been a "good soldier" and should go out "by any honorable means"—this meant, my father explained to me, that my uncle had my father's blessing to shoot himself, as his father had done. My uncle, however, died naturally, if quite painfully.

Sometimes it seems to me that ice water ran in my father's veins, rather than blood: to hear him tell the breath-by-breath version of my brother's last moments, for example, of how the inhalations grew slower and slower and then finally stopped (he and my mother had been called to the hospital in the middle of the night; I was too far away)—here he paused each time in the re-telling to imitate the sound of my brother's breaths—makes me think he is a zombie. Regarding his own death, which he says he believes to be the end of it all, my father is utterly dispassionate. Still, he wanted a funeral befitting a soldier, and his gravestone to read "COL MAURICE C. FLEMING, AUS [the correct form to designate Army of the United States]." And I knew just how the flag was to be spread, and how it was to be handed to me: my father went over every detail.

According to family report, my paternal grandfather was a tyrant who kept his wife in her place by threats and terrorized the two sons, whom he planned to keep on the farm to work in the fields. Sons, it seemed, should never have more education than the father. Apparently my grandmother surprised them all by not only having, but expressing, contrary views. The fact that she had inherited a bit of money in her own name allowed her the freedom to defy her husband, on this one issue at least: her children were going to go to college. After scraping together the nerve to cross him this once, however, she apparently had shot her wad, and never did so again. Perhaps she saw better than her husband that subsistence farming was doomed as a way of life. Or perhaps she was motivated by a love of learning, or at least a respect for it: she belonged to a generation, or perhaps a class, of people, for whom respect was a more powerful motivator than love.

My father therefore enrolled in Western Maryland College, a small liberal-arts college north of Baltimore that, he told me once, he had confused with the state university because of the fact that "Maryland" appears in both of their names. Nowadays he would certainly be savvier, and at any rate would have no basis for confusion: the college has changed its name to "McDaniel College" and begun a relentless advertising campaign in the Baltimore area.

Recently he gave me the silver napkin ring he used with the linen napkins in the college dining hall, remnant of a vanished world. Linen in a college dining hall! Silver! And once he showed me his college yearbook; what he was proudest of was a drawing that served as the title page for the local ROTC unit: he explained to me that he was the model for this silhouette of the well-built, chest-out/shoulders-back young soldier. I suppose the yearbook is among his effects, and that one day I will be its owner. Will I keep it out of a sense of duty? And for how long?

Decay

The form my father's "reversion" took was to embrace failure, decay, and pessimism with open arms. I can see the advantages for my father of proceeding like this. Even if it requires blighting the hopes and projects of all those around you, which I sincerely believe was not a factor for my blinkered (Asperger's?) father, such a world-view renders life logical: even what appear to be momentary upswings are simply waiting to turn down. Pessimism is as defensible a world-view as optimism, which for its part is the belief that setbacks, rather than upswings, are temporary. Pessimism, in a mirror-image version, asserts that apparent successes are merely awaiting their reverse. My mother, in later years, had the theory that my father wanted everyone to live at the same subsistence level he himself had lived at, in the farmhouse in Somerset County with the outhouse and cold-water pump, the constant fight against poverty that occasionally won, the sandy soil and the tyrant father. The purpose would have been to make others as miserable as he was himself, so as to prove to himself that no one was better than he.

After his retirement from Salisbury State University, as it was then, where he was ultimately moved from the Biology Department to administration to the Education Department in an effort to find a place where he would have the least interaction with students, he took to riding military airplanes on a "space available" basis. He'd go to Dover Air Force Base, an hour away, and ask where the next airplane was going. Then he'd get on it. He went everywhere, from Thailand to Diego Garcia to Germany. The soldiers saw his ID that proclaimed him a Colonel, and called him "sir." In my mother's opinion, this was the real point of the exercise—he had tried to get Keith and me to call him "sir" years before, and failed. I can see it from his point of view: certainly riding an airplane and spending a few nights in a BOQ in U.S. Base Wherever beat sitting alone in his rooms in Salisbury, Maryland. He would spend the night, perhaps take a bus tour of the local city if one was available for a price he held to be reasonable, and turn around and come home. In this way he "saw" the world, from Bangkok to Europe. He filled a very fat passport with visa stamps, and was proud of the passport. Getting stamps in it was another part of the exercise.

Traveling is said to broaden, and so it was with my father. At least it was useful in the development of his theories. He always waxed poetic on the state of the world when the oil runs out: we will all be on bicycles, like the people he had seen in Thailand on one of these trips. Once home, my father spent his time polishing his theories of world civilization, all of which had the common end of a total collapse of the global economy. I heard them without variation for over a decade. Perhaps my mother was right: Thailand on bicycles looked like his youth. The whole world was to be like Somerset County, Maryland, Anno Domini 1924, the year he was ten.

The polishing of my father's theories was, to him, its own end, as if he had spent hours cleaning a tombstone or re-arranging the pebbles in his garden. They were the gimcrack theories of a village *racconteur* who was his own final arbiter. From my point of view, they were below freshman level thinking, riddled with fallacies. During the period when once again I was willing to talk with him, I interacted by offering the most basic objections to his theories, gleaned from the daily newspapers or recollected from undergraduate economics classes. He was always astonished that I "knew so much."

Years later I thought of these elaborate weed-choked theories of my father as I stood before an astonishing assemblage that found its final resting place in the National Museum of American Art in Washington. Usually called for the sake of brevity "The Throne of the Third Heaven" (the name goes on and on from there) it's the decades-long garage construction, by a Washington man named James Hampton, of a monument to and worship space for a private religion dubiously related to Christianity. What the viewer sees is a room-filling glistening assemblage of aluminum foil-covered chairs decorated with knobs and spandrels and with a huge "throne" in the middle, a chair gleaming with the kitchen foil so lovingly applied over so many years. There are accompanying inspired writings, but they're all written in an invented language, and incomprehensible.

As an oddity, it's pretty amusing. As a religious statement, it's a bust, since religion by definition is publicly shared belief. No one can decipher the writings, and the assemblage just looks like the by-product of obsession. It seems incredible that anyone did all this. Yet to the creator, it was an expression of objective reality, the True Faith. That's the way it always is with gigantic individual constructions like this that never have to knock against the rest of the world. They can grow all sorts of weird shoots that are never pruned. To be sure, all the rest of the world that has to be pruned ends up looking pretty much alike. That's why we put these lush creepy weed growths in museums: they're something different. Useless, of course, but different.

Nobody but me ever objected to my father's theories, and if I hadn't, they would have continued to send out their tendrils. Probably they did anyway. For him, at any rate, they served their purpose. As publicly defendable theses rather than a private religion, they were useless. I bet James Hampton's "Throne" kept him happy too, not to mention busy. It's a metaphor for all our lives, except that we can regard it with envy: neither Hampton nor my father had to put up with the world telling him "no" as all the rest of us do.

Ivy League

My perspective on my father's role in my childhood is limited by the fact that I was, in fact, a child. It surprised me years later when my mother, who for a time occasionally invited my father to her house for dinner when Alexandra and I were going to be there, mentioned that she had thought of having him over for Christmas dinner.

"So is he coming?" I asked.

"No," she said. "I couldn't bring myself to do it. He ruined too many Christmases for me."

I can even feel charitable, now that I'm not subjected to them, regarding his endless intolerable tirades about how stupid most of the politicians are, how the advertisers are only out to trick people's money out of their pockets, and how most people don't think before they speak. At the time, I would have given anything to have spared my mother, and us, listening to all this. And certainly they grew old the hundredth time, even probably by the fourth or fifth. But at this distance I can at least say: they're all true. And the most fundamental truth of all is this: our world is full of people spending vast amounts of money to get people to do things that are bad for them. Be suspicious: it's the only way to get through life alive.

At the same time, the suspiciousness I imbibed in the air surrounding my father's tirades may have lulled me into a false sense of security regarding my ability to take care of myself. When, newly returned from Africa and in the early years of my marriage, I found that I had moved heaven and earth to marry a woman who fed her children Wonder Bread and Coca-Cola and left them for hours in front of the television set, who had no idea where the garbage went when it left the curb and asked me one day, in all innocence, whether the Greeks or the Romans came first, I felt as if I had willingly chopped off my own hands and ground them up for hamburger, using my feet to turn the crank.

What am I to make of things when later, in what appeared to be a rejection of his former ways, my father wrote checks for tens of thousands of dollars for the house I lived in when married, and again the house I live in now? When I remember of the heartache over a dollar, over a dime, when I was ten, and multiply that by multiples of thousands, it seems that I hold the whole sum of human misery in my hand with his checks. But of course, that was then and this is now. Back then a dollar was his way to control us. Now it's only money.

The biggest fight over money came when my brother, the day it was announced that he was our high school's only National Merit Semi-Finalist, told my father that he wanted to go to the University of Pennsylvania. My father, still bathing in the glow of his own reflected glory, agreed. Anything my brother wanted, he would have. My brother disappeared into the den to work on the application. An hour or so later my father appeared in the doorway, a drink in his hand: my brother wasn't sending the application. A private university was money down the drain. Keith would go to the University of Maryland. And he did.

I wonder if Keith might have taken a different course if he had gone to Ivy-League Penn rather than to then-mediocre Maryland: somehow, I doubt it. He would, in all probability, have been just as unable to express his feelings, my father would have pressured him just as much to become a dentist while he was figuring out that he wanted to be a musician, he would have been just as confused about his sexuality in a world that wanted him to put his penis in girls' vaginas while he was figuring out he'd rather stick his fist up men's behinds.

So what if he flunked all his science courses at Maryland? That he racked up a sheaf of nearly a thousand dollars worth of campus parking tickets because he was too lazy to walk to the lot further from his dorm for which he had a valid sticker, tickets which doubled and trebled in price and which my mother ended up having to pay before he could get his diploma? That he very nearly didn't get any diploma at all, given his unwillingness to pass a simple piano exam, once he was a music major—an exam which, three years after he should have graduated, was simply, miraculously, done away with, allowing him to get his degree?

This is the particular form his recalcitrance took in the life he led. Who's to say it wouldn't have taken other forms in another life? As it is, after he was years out of college he continued running up appalling bills for thousands of dollars worth of vinyl records, which he bought almost as if addicted. He didn't want to stand in line in the (admittedly appallingly inefficient) District of Columbia car registration facilities, and got hundreds of dollars worth of tickets for being without a residential parking sticker for his own neighborhood, or for having an expired one, or for failing to have his car inspected. Periodically the tickets would mount up, through the miracle of time-doubling, to the point where his car would be towed to the Brentwood impound lot on seamy New York Avenue. Mother rescued it several times. She even paid the bills when he ran short of money to pay the rent: out of guilt, she later said, that she had given in to my father. Probably he always knew she would.

Nowadays we speak of "enablers." My mother was clearly Keith's enabler. She was destined to be Margaret Thatcher but had to settle for being a music professor at a small college, which left plenty of organizational capabilities unused. They had to go in some direction or other. When we were little, they went towards us. Now, once again, they are channeled towards my children: for many years I stepped aside, wishing I could do so more successfully and with a better humor, not taking each time, as I invariably did, as a personal affront her countermanding my own plans.

How predestined are we to end as we do? And how soon? Was Keith's life, which ended in a spiraling death from AIDS, in some sense inevitable, his self-destruction working itself out in his sexual carelessness well after everyone was well aware of how people caught what we now call HIV?

When I went to Africa, in 1985, there were even some respected scientists who refused to rule out transmission from mosquitoes, and saliva. I of course read everything I could about AIDS. I even got myself vaccinated for Hepatitis B because a French friend of mine had a doctor buddy who insisted on the connection between Hepatitis B and AIDS. My friend told me this a month before I was to leave for Rwanda; I got the first in the three-shot series, meant to be spaced a month apart, the next day, the second the day before I left, and took the third with me, on ice, into the Air France to Kigali.

Even I knew all the prostitutes were infected, that it was relatively difficult for a man to get it through vaginal intercourse with a woman, and that a condom could effectively block transmission. And still I had myself tested twice, by a doctor at the Embassy. So of course I asked Keith, on my return from Rwanda, if he had been tested.

"What difference would it make?" he asked, in his "I don't want to talk about this" tone of voice. And that was that.

If it hadn't been AIDS that got him it would, it seems, have been something else—he seems to have been an accident waiting to happen. Or is this merely Monday morning quarterbacking, confusing the real with the inevitable? Certainly when we have ended, it all seems logical, but is this not merely an expression of our rage for order, the desire to say that it really all did make sense, somehow?

Precious church

My parents fought that night in the kitchen over my brother's choice of colleges, while my brother and I sat on the stairs and listened. My father threatened to divorce her, "and then you'll *never* get back into your precious church."

At the time, that seemed a potent threat. My mother fought, then gave in, for what she says was the last time. From then on, the split widened, and she increasingly went her own way. When finally she sought the Church's opinion on her impending divorce, it turned out that she had nothing to worry about. Since she wasn't married to her husband, in the Church's eyes, a divorce was not only not a divorce, but a sign of good faith that she "wanted to get out of the relationship." She would have only to obtain the civil divorce, then go to confession, noting of course along the way that she had lived in sin for thirty years and had two illegitimate children. When she told me all this, I was both amused and appalled. My mother saw the humor of the situation too, but ultimately did as she had been told, going to a priest who knew the story, did not press her for details, and was, in short, the soul of humanity and discretion.

At fifty-something, therefore, she formally re-entered the Church that had excommunicated her decades before. At first she made up for lost time, going every morning to Mass; with time things settled down to once a week. My mother is a believer, convinced, she says cheerily, that the afterlife is a reality. Does this conviction come from her own childhood, as my skepticism comes from mine?

Penny loafers

It is a well known fact that loafer shoes do not give the same kind of arch support as oxford tie-ups. Nowadays, everybody wears running shoes even when they aren't running, so this is no longer the burning junior-high issue it once was (now in most places Middle Schools). My mother, a paragon of good sense and unwillingness to be controlled by mob mentality, insisted we wear tie-up shoes. The problem was that everybody else was wearing scuffed brown penny-loafers with shiny pennies in them. Everybody had them—everybody, that is, at the high school in Salisbury, Maryland, which defined (or attempted to define) my world—and so, I imagine, in its thousands of clones in small towns across the country. Of course, I wanted penny loafers too.

Then there was the completely justifiable refusal of my mother, no spendthrift (to this day she diligently clips coupons and buys things on sale, most of which come in very handy for me), to pay for those expensive oxford-cloth shirts with useless hanger-loops outside on the back, denominated at the time "fairy loops," that the really popular girls snipped (if allowed), or tore off for their collection albums. Memory here does not lie, I believe, though seen at the remove of many decades, this seems even more absurd than most teen-aged absurdities.

More fundamental than mere aberrations of clothing was the fact that, having skipped second grade, Keith and I were a year younger than our classmates. Thus it was when I entered the third grade that I met my now-ex-wife; here, I'll call her Martha. She was in school with me up to senior year in high school. As a result of being younger, I was the last boy in gym class to develop pubic hair, the weakest in the rope climb, the last in the races. I can still remember collapsing on the parallel bars, my arms buckling.

For all my father talked about bodies in his biology classes, my brother and I might as well not have had them. Completely unphysical himself, save for the sex he apparently enjoyed so greatly, he was as distant and unphysical with his sons as a frog. Or was he over-compensating in some way for his childhood in which physicality was a necessary way of life, not something to be sought as recreation? If so, it was the only way that he ever rejected his childhood. Not once, at any rate, did he ever play ball, run, lift weights, or roughhouse with his two sons. Is it for this reason that I have turned into such a gym rat? That I was for so long so desperate for a son to do all these things with?

I suppose it's a revenge of sorts that I think nothing of running six miles carrying twenty pounds excess weight first thing in the morning, or that I sport a 6'2" designer body with a 44" chest, a 32" waist, and 16" arms—exactly the Greeks' idea of perfect proportions. Yet what a limp revenge this is, this revenge on a past that doesn't know it's being revenged upon.

And why should memory be so important anyway? So much of my own life has faded with time, and I have no madeleine to bring it back—and no belief that anything would be proven if it did. But did that mean my life didn't exist? Why should Proust have been so exultant at getting back the past? What if he forgot it again? What if he hadn't written it down? Why should memory redeem the past if living it failed to be enough by itself?

Bicycle

I rode around the decaying downtown of Salisbury, Maryland, finding what may have been an objective correlative to myself in the rusting bridge over the oil-slicked river, the fading jackets and suits in the thrift shop of one of the churches, in a musty shop down a side street, in the dusty panes of all but defunkt drugstores, in the glowing tackiness of the Woolworth's. The discovery of a plaque dedicating a copse of trees on the college campus to some students who had died stayed with me for months. The world was permeated, it seemed, with death, a thought new to a reflective 14-year-old.

I liked riding halfway across town, a treacherous journey at lights across highways, to bring back tropical fish in clear plastic bags slipped into crisp brown paper ones. The fish contributed to the warm humidity of my room with its rows of tanks and the small animals in cages, all with their puzzling belief that being out of their natural element of tank or cage was better than being in—which invariably led to death by dessication for the fish and an adventuresome several days for the small animals. I knew after a time that I should only open the cage door and put it on the floor; in the middle of the night the next night, or the next, or the next, I would hear the squeak, squeak, squeak of the wheel and sneak stealthily out of bed to pounce on the cage and close the door.

I created miniature worlds: I remember laboriously making a terrarium as a birthday present for my mother in the workroom of the neighbor's garage, and then being devastated when I arrived from vacation a week later to find the tiny perfection of the plants, the pool made of a bottle cap, the hillock of moss, all gone to seed, dried up, grown gangly, or dead: in the moment I had left it it had been so perfect. Yet even adults make this mistake of thinking that a natural arrangement will be permanent: later, in my commuter marriage year with Meg, living up the road from the Lawrenceville School in New Jersey, I remember reading with interest that the landscaping for the school, by Central Park architect Olmstead, had envisioned the trees at nineteenth century levels. With time, they had far outgrown the houses and buildings they now dwarfed, rendering visually incomprehensible the so-carefully planned arrangement: apparently Olmstead hadn't calculated for change and growth either.

Other sensations come back in memory: there was the chinchilla-soft dust on the floor of the dilapidated garage that, when stirred up, made columns of whiteness that the sun cut in grimy transverse columns through the air. There was the naked slope of a neighbor's yard that I raked, over and over, revealing the limp too-long pale grass that had grown under the layer of damp leaves I was removing. There was the tiny flying squirrel salvaged after a hurricane that littered the front yard with limbs, fed on an eye dropper for a few days but not destined for long life. There was the tiny flashlight, probably a keychain, I got for some Christmas that made me feel like one of the Hardy Boys, wearing a sweater I thought look liked theirs, Frank and Joe and their "pals," my wish-fulfillment heroes of mid-elementary school.

I had found my own coping mechanism, by about the tenth grade, in Bohemianism, arriving in school in used clothing from the thrift store wearing long woolen scarves that draped down to the floor. I followed admiringly from afar as the few students from my high school who had managed to get into "good" colleges protested the war, smoked dope, and led the life of the 60s. It was, I suppose, ironic that by the time I got to college the 60s were over, if not the Vietnam War, and I discovered that what I really wanted to do with my time was read books rather than protest.

I had been categorized, or had packaged myself for others' categorization, as the unathletic intellectual aesthete of the school. This meant that the only girlfriends I had were in the summers, when I went to music camp (I was a violinist) and entered other worlds where I could be judged by what I was rather than what others saw in me. (Another possibility is: where the girls were more interesting.) One reason my ego refused to shrivel and die is that I discovered that girls liked me fine. The inevitable pimples aside, I was tall and apparently not unattractive. I remember endless make-out sessions in the woods (this at a music camp in the Western Maryland mountains) with a girl named Rhetta who had long dark hair, sessions that made the spit dribble down our chins and of course threatened to explode my pants. Still, I was too shy to "go all the way," or even to ask her to touch me below the belt. This I had to do for myself later, in the rustic bathroom stall of the bunk house. And then in the dormitory at West Virginia University, where I went to a subsequent music camp, I continued the summer make-outs and began intensely cerebral platonic affairs with "older" (read: college age) women who made me feel grown up but who did not, somehow, take the initiative of popping my cherry. It might have been the late 60s in the cities, but where I was it was still firmly 1954.

Back at school in Salisbury, I never overcame the conviction that there at least, I could look at girls but, unlike the other boys, was not allowed to touch. Probably the emotional correlate to this, at least with respect to Martha, who was my friend through high school, was that I idealized her horribly. When, many years later as an adult, she showed her sexual side, it seemed like entering fascinating territory, eating fruit not so much forbidden as hidden in plain sight. If I'd had a fling with Martha at sixteen, I think, I could have gotten it out of my system and avoided a lot of nonsense about marriage later on. But if I had been able to have an affair, I would have been a completely different person than I was.

Purgatory

High school for Keith was certainly an even more intense purgatory than for me. Surely he must have sensed a lack of attraction to girls; so far as I know he never slept with a woman. He must have been even more isolated than I, and played the part of the nerd to compensate. Only more recently, by reading *Becoming a Man,* Paul Monette's excruciating, angry, and beautifully-written memoir of growing up gay and closeted, have I begun to understand what life must have been like for my brother, and begun to forgive him. Monette's memories of himself were the Keith that I saw: the shying away from personal relationships, his limp-wristed "nelly-boy" imitations and jokes about gay men or men who seemed effeminate, jokes that continued well into college. It made me accept Freud's intuition that people make jokes about things that worry them; telling a joke is scratching an itch that will never heal. Did Keith also suffer from the crushes on his peers that Monette chronicles? It would humanize him to me if I thought he did. But of this I saw no evidence; of course I wasn't meant to. Part of me suspects he had killed even the feelings. This can't be true; I shudder to think that his emotional armor reached as deeply into his being as this.

Living with Keith, who put up such a battle against the truth of his own sexuality, made several other things clear to me as well. The dream of clarity about ourselves and other people is only a dream. How much error we are constantly in even—or especially—with respect to ourselves! We think we want A, and in fact years later decide what we really want is B. Or should this read, that we really wanted (in the past tense) B, even when we were saying A? Are we wrong about ourselves or do we merely change? Who's to say? And this shows us once again that the illusion of the world being infinitely decidable, infinitely clear if only we can get it to talk, is only that: an illusion. We shouldn't have had to wait for Heisenberg's Uncertainty Principle to realize that most of the world is neither decidable nor decided: we don't even question most of it, and what we do question doesn't necessarily give us truthful answers.

Of course Keith's self-denial may have been extreme. Concluding that everyone is as out of touch with himself as Keith, for many years, clearly was, may be drawing too large a generalization. Or was he merely like a scientist with a theory he wants to hold onto at any cost, despite the mounting pile of counter-evidence. At first they may plausibly be held to be quirks, or exceptions; at a certain point, however, they must be acknowledged to disprove the theory.

Keith and I were alike in finding all this high school nonsense quite ridiculous, as of course I did from the time I was about 14. It served at least to make us close, give us something in common. Past high school we drifted apart. Even through the time when we lived together during my early twenties, each of us led separate lives. When Keith subsequently moved into Washington with his first boyfriend Michael who I believe finally pulled him physically from the closet, our lives diverged past compatibility. (I'd bet that Keith said no many times to Michael before realizing that, in fact, no did mean yes.)

Not that we didn't continue to see each other. But I was elsewhere, and we saw each other infrequently. Our talk was limited to references to the past; Keith never willingly shared his hopes and dreams, his feelings or his frustrations. Michael finally left Keith (as he told me later) because he couldn't stand the isolation of living with Keith and having so little emotional contact. Or was it Keith's promiscuity during his leather-bar phase that hurt him more? His last roommate before the hospital phase that was the slippery slope to death, gay but not a lover, was driven crazy by the dildos in the dishwasher: Keith was anything but considerate.

I can see that he was going through some of the same body-perception battles that I subsequently went through, though (as was characteristic of him), in extreme fashion, and inconsistently. I'm sure that he too, like me, had to (as we now say) "give himself permission" to get the body he wanted. For a time he worked on losing his adult flab, went to the gym relentlessly, and turned into a mass of muscle, a fireplug with lats that he showed off with skin-tight t-shirts, some of which I still have today. I threw away the obscene ones, and they're plenty tight on me, even with my longer, slimmer body. I wonder how he could breathe.

It was during this phase he must have been heaviest into his promiscuous phase. I know about the leather, because the first time he was in the hospital my mother finally broke open the lock on the storage room in his basement and discovered his dungeon, as I've since learned it's called: an arrangement of leather swings, chains, slings, and trays of shining silver balls. I got a crash course against my will in what Keith did there when the Polaroid photographs slid out in a pile from a credenza he had on his nightstand. At this point Keith wasn't dead yet, but his house was being cleaned out, as he was flat on his back on a cot in my mother's living room, and had been so for months. There was my brother in a black hood, his chest criss-crossed with chains, his arm up to the elbow in another man's ass. (That's where the silver balls go too, it seems.)

My mother cleaned out the dungeon, though technically it wasn't her property, in a gesture of re-establishing control over my brother, or perhaps disgust. Among the things she found were cans of Crisco, I assume lubricant (the photographs suggested as much), each neatly labeled with a man's name. Was this labeling a disease-prevention mechanism? Or merely territory-marking? If the former, Keith can't have been so careful in other circumstances. For of course one can't get AIDS by either putting one's arm up another man's rectum, or by having it done. It's perfectly safe sex.

The muscle phase didn't last long, and in a matter of years Keith was overweight again, from his constant diet of Big Macs and chocolate, and losing his hair. If Keith had been able to talk, to break out of his prison, to open up to someone, he would not, I like to think, have been so self-destructive. But if he had been different, he wouldn't have been Keith. All of us are onions: remove all our layers and we cease to exist. Which doesn't mean we can't change specific layers. But would I want to change our past, if that were possible, to have things have been other than they were? I'm happy with what I've become; at least I have accepted it, learning to turn my unavoidable weaknesses to good effect.

Could I have the same personality without the pain of outsidership that produced it? If I had had a childhood marked not by alienation but by congruence with my surroundings of age, speech pattern, sensibility—in short, all those things that separated me from the world—might there not still have been a core of me that would have rebelled anyway, and that with much greater difficulty and much later in life? Would I, raised wearing penny loafers and watching television, have been happy? Or would I have been unhappy without having the objective correlative that would enable me to articulate why? I can describe, I can explain, but not for an instant do I think that I am thereby any closer to understanding.

Two

Glory in the Flower

Alma mater

For my first year of college, I went to the Honors Program at Maryland, my state university, before transferring to Haverford. Ironically, Maryland was the school that my father had forced Keith to go to. Maryland gave me a scholarship, as I was in my turn a National Merit Finalist, but that's not why I went: I went because I was wait-listed at one college and turned down flat by the other two to which I had applied, and whose "yes, of course, come," I had simply taken for granted. I knew I didn't fit in in my high school; I thought I'd identified the world where I did belong, the world that would welcome with open arms. But belonging somewhere and having others acknowledge it turned out to be two different things.

I imagine their reactions had something to do with the essay I wrote that must have seemed offensive (it said something about "Nazi boots")—I knew it wasn't scores, grades, or recommendations. Too many people from the Eastern Shore of Maryland applying that year? I couldn't have found out why even then and I'll certainly never find out now: this is too far back in the shifting sands, and there's no path back. I remember coming home from Washington from violin and cello lessons to find the first rejection. I lay rigid on the bed that night for hours. What could this mean? That I wasn't what I thought I was? The second "no" arrived a day or two later, and then the wait-list for the third. I went through hell for a week or so, picking up the pieces of my shattered self. That was the first time I had to do this; the second and more disturbing one was in the years after college. This first time the foundations of the world shook was useful training for the next few years, when the world told me "no" a lot. Finally I realized the world doesn't know what it wants, or should want, is bored, inattentive, or isn't a "world" at all. All it means is that you find other ways to get what you want: you do your pitch, the person you're pitching says "no," you say "thank you for your time," collect your belongings, and leave to find someone else. That's not the run-up to life, it is life.

This experience also made me realize that the fact that everybody wants one particular thing, or place, usually turns out to mean that there are dozens of equally good alternatives they're ignoring. I thought this a year later in Paris, which turned out to be every bit as fun a place to be as the New York I had somehow never managed to be part of. And it's individuals doing something the rest of the world isn't doing that render the meanest provincial corner interesting for those who come later: Santa Fe now touts Georgia O'Keefe as a museum draw, and every one of the otherwise uninteresting stops on Van Gogh's descent into death in both northern and southern France has become a tourist destination, complete with billboard-sized reproductions of his paintings set in the very fields and before the very church he depicted. You look from the painting afflicted by gigantism and then at the field it's marooned in: somehow the juxtaposition is supposed to teach you something. That's the silver lining: if everyone is lined up at one bank teller, it means the others are free.

Besides, after a certain age, there's no point in remembering all the things in our lives that don't work out the way we think they will—for most of us, after a few years, there are just too many to keep track. Think how many failures we would have to record, if we recorded them all. Every line of my personal and professional CV has behind it a row of ghosts, trembles with the faint cries of the unborn that had to remain so in order for actuality to come to fruition. For that reason it's useful to remind others that they're there, so they don't think they're the only ones with all these ghostly failures in their closets.

Behind every article entry I see the shadows of the journals that did not publish it, beside my degrees the places I was rejected by. Even changes of plan count as things that didn't happen: behind my University of Chicago M.A. is the fact that when I went there I thought I'd stay for a Ph.D. and was finally so miserable I left, going for two years to the University of Munich before looking for a graduate program that would pay me: Vanderbilt was the answer (UCLA, I suddenly remember, said no: add that to the shadow-CV). Not to mention, oh yes, the rejection from the MFA Creative Writing Program after college. That one I barely noticed: I didn't want to be told what to write and had applied because others seemed to think it a good idea.

Nobody sees the things that didn't happen; people see the path we do take, not the countless ones we don't. I moved into a dormitory room at Maryland with Keith knowing I'd transfer after a year. I played the violin in the university symphony and gorged on double burgers, fries, onion rings, fried chicken, things I've learned since to regard with horror. The classes in the Honors Program, it turned out, were the academic equal of any I subsequently had at Haverford: I took economics and philosophy with the other Honors students, who were bright people who could not afford or who, like me, had not gotten into the school they had wanted. The next time around I was careful to be less flip on the essays. This time around, the Ivy League said yes—but by then I wanted something smaller, and by then I knew about the Teaching Assistants who taught most large classes at large universities. I went to Haverford.

I liked Haverford, but only for a year or so. I found was that my dream of sophisticated, witty people at "good colleges" was a mirage. They existed, there and at our sister school, Bryn Mawr, but I didn't have the time or energy to waste with them. Wit was a hollow show. I was too interested in my own mental journey. I realized too that the interesting people who give outside aura or cachet to famous places aren't interacting with each other. In fact, they're probably ignoring each other. They're too full of themselves. It's only outsiders or people with no goals who see them as a totality, and the place itself as interesting. Gertrude Stein famously boycotted James Joyce in our mythical "Paris of the '20s." Besides, if you'd walked the streets in 1925 you wouldn't have sensed "Paris of the '20s," you'd have been concentrating on getting to your meeting, or wondering what to have for lunch.

Tractatus

At Maryland, I had devoured Adam Smith and John Maynard Keynes and dreamed of going on to the London School of Economics. After a time, however, I realized that economics could tell us how to allocate goods and resources, but it couldn't say why, or to whom. A course in social philosophers—Bentham, Marx, John Rawls—had convinced me that only philosophy held the answers to this question. What I discovered at Haverford was that it didn't. Philosophy wasn't an accretive process, but a starting-from-zero each time a new major thinker came along to contradict his predecessor. What we were studying was precisely people who would never agree (the ones who agreed too much weren't major thinkers), and so who could not, collectively speaking, point us in any particular direction.

Wittgenstein, and Wittgenstein alone, seemed to have put his finger on the problem with philosophy, and, in the *Tractatus*, attempted to say once and for all (leaving out the technical difficulties of the "picture theory of meaning") why philosophy didn't go anywhere. I spent hours poring over this text, in *face-en-face* English and German (which I was also taking, a new language for me). I had the sense of being carried somewhere where I deeply longed to go and had not even imagined existed, as if someone were speaking for me. Wittgenstein was right: philosophy went nowhere, not even to the *Investigations*, which seemed to me a defeated work, a kind of lengthy series of P.S.'s, fragments instead of the attempt, however futile, to construct a system. Which is what he said about it too.

Besides, I was fed up with being told what to read. Read this, take this test: I was too conscious of having to do well not to do as I was told, so I dropped the book I really wanted to read in favor of the course whose test was looming. Having read St. Augustine's *Confessions*, I wanted to go on to the *City of God*. But when? I had to put it aside for, say, my Baroque History course. It seemed so dry, this business of "taking courses," as if one were a boat that could be buffeted about by whatever wind picked one up rather than being allowed to gather speed on one's own. Now, I realize that most people don't gather speed on their own—so being told what to do, what to read, what to study for, is an alternative only to being dead in the water. To me it was like being a mouse played with by a cat: swatted in this direction, and then that, when all I really wanted was to get away with a library and a constant source of food to work my way through both.

Either I could drop out of college, or I could finish up quickly. By taking six classes a semester and using my Advanced Placement credit, I left Haverford after two years with a diploma, and with the firm resolve that I was done with other people educating me—which in practice meant, telling me what to read and when to stop reading it. By then what I wanted to do was write, just have the time to make something out of the bits and pieces I had begun that fall and spring.

I had, of course, friends during my time at Haverford, but I was so wrapped in the cocoon of my own thoughts, it's not clear that anybody could have had much of an effect on me. I had a very cerebral friendship with a very intelligent pianist. He was my closest friend; others were more peripheral. The friendship faltered when, after a year, he told me he was gay, though we lurched through my last year there, having decided that this had no effect on our enjoyment of each others' conversation. Somehow it ended up doing so anyhow. The weekend after I graduated from college, I moved into Keith's one-bedroom apartment in what was then the blue-collar suburban Washington community of Chillum Heights. Keith was away for the summer at Meadowmount, the music camp in the Adirondacks then run by Ivan Galamian of Juilliard. My mother was taking courses at Catholic University for a degree in Religious Education. I was to cat-sit Papageno, Keith's bird-catching feline of more than usual intelligence. And write.

The urgency of my desire to do this, just to have the world at bay so I could develop my own work, is what now seems so touching. It really seemed to me as if art could change the world. In college, finishing up courses and exams and knowing it would soon be over, I counted almost literally the minutes, certainly the days, until I could begin to work again, to relieve the vast pressure of this force that roiled within me, addressing sense of being pregnant with a huge thing that only I could extrude from my body. All I wanted was for the world to leave me alone to embark on my private odyssey.

Still, it was terrifying, though essential. Would I have the talent?

Years later I saw a short movie with Dirk Bogarde based on a Somerset Maugham short story, both called "The Alien Corn." In it, the golden boy son of a wealthy family wants to be a pianist. The family makes a bargain with him: he can study in Paris for a time, but must agree that when that time is over he will come back and let a great pianist say whether or not he possesses talent. If the answer is yes, he may go on. If not, he must give in to the father's desire to join the family business. He does all this; the verdict is negative: the verdict is that he plays mechanically and with no talent. The young man, much to his family's surprise and horror, shoots himself. Over such a thing! They can't understand this at all. I of course understood completely.

Beyond Watergate

That first Monday I drove to the University of Maryland library, which I had left two years before, found a congenial carrel, opened my notebook with its childlike lined paper, and picked up my work where I had been forced to leave it at college—there I'd managed to write perhaps twenty pages. Some five experimental works and more than two years later, I left this library again, this time for good. More than twenty years after the fact, the first of the books I wrote during this time appeared with a small press: *Twilley,* a book begun when I was still in college, and finished in the bowels of an over-air-conditioned library. It sold a few thousand copies, was compared flatteringly by a handful of perhaps too erudite reviewers to works by Thoreau, Proust, Henry James, T.S. Eliot, and the film director David Lynch, and has otherwise disappeared. It typed out initially at 600 pages, and was published at 300. When I went to edit it as an adult, I had realized that not everything a nineteen-year-old thought interesting or funny seemed so to an adult, and realized as well that virtually no one else but me—or more to the point, my nineteen-year-old self—had the attention span necessary to reading sentences three and four pages long.

In the time between writing and publication, there was an M.A., a Ph.D., a Fulbright, teaching in Germany and Rwanda, many scholarly books and countless articles, a falling in love and marriage and a daughter. Also trial by a bipolar step-daughter, a falling out of love followed by an acrimonious divorce, and my brother's death. And then the problems with my daughter, the necessity of getting along with my ex if I wanted to continue to see my daughter. And then later: re-marriage, first one son and then another. By any standards, a life, if life is really what happens while we're doing something else. A life that, unlike a tragedy with a beginning, middle, and end, has to have order imposed upon it if it's to have any order at all, at least the order of seeing that it led to now.

I tried out different writing spots for the first week or so. By the second week, I had found "my" place, to which I went each day. Apparently no one else wanted it, at least not at that hour of the morning. It was a glass-enclosed room that I think was meant to be turned ultimately into an audio listening room and had somehow been left unfinished: there was a desk with several holes cut in it, I assume for wires. Outside the room, as the months went by, the Watergate hearings played on monitors in a discussion area of the library: I passed them in the morning and at night. What did the President know and when did he know it? I was too lost in my own internal drama to care.

Our apartment development, that I left every morning and to which I returned every night, was striking in its very averageness. At the time this area outside of Washington was largely populated by blue-collar white people, the apartments the refuge of the unattached and of young families. It was neither ugly nor beautiful: agreeable, but plain, one of the innumerable brick-box "garden apartment" complexes built during the 1960s, made different only by being right across the street from the greenery of the sports fields and from two huge surreal gas balloons that rose and fell in their equally huge circular girders as the months went on, sometimes filling the horizon, sometimes leaving behind only their empty nest.

This very averageness, coupled with this so-functional surrealism of the gas balloons, was the source of its beauty, like a quotidian version of William Eggleston photographs. I loved the apartment complex's parking lots of black asphalt that become steamy with the summer heat, brick outsides, aluminum windows, white-painted walls. I even loved, because from a distance, the people who lived in them, the older widows with their birdcage hair, the teenagers leaning against the cars at night, the windows open to the summer air with the far-off sound of radios. It was the melancholy of the ordinary, so much sadder than the melancholy of the grandiose.

Though it was sultry Washington D.C. summer outside, at least when I first started writing, it was cold in my room with an unrelenting thermostat-controlled cold. By the end of the day, after eight nearly motionless hours with only my thermos of coffee, I was glad to emerge into steamy air. I knew I would begin to feel hungry during the afternoon, and looked forward to the feeling of sharpness it produced. That summer I lost the twenty pounds of flab I had put on at college, sitting over countless ice creams and coffee after meals with the group I hung out with because we wanted to keep up our so-witty banter that covered everything and nothing.

I slept, ate, dressed, spoke to the neighbors, argued with Keith, and wrote. This life went on for almost two years, and sputtered out in a third. The friends I had were borrowed ones, Keith's, as he worked on an M.A. and then Ph.D. at Catholic University. Somewhere in the middle of this the University of Maryland removed its piano requirement, which Keith had stubbornly refused to fulfill, though any sane person would merely have bitten the bullet and done it, and he graduated from college, by mail. I wouldn't have wanted any friends of my own: they would have taken too much time. Now, two marriages and three children later (not counting my first marriage's stepchildren), this is not a life I can conceive of, or even hope to render comprehensible to an outsider, or even to myself. Indeed, it was possible at all only for someone momentarily de-coupled from the reality of the world, set free to follow out to its end a trajectory of internal definition.

Shapes and sounds

Yet, I can at least say: I too have been in Arcadia. I know, as I think few people do know, what it is to live at full intellectual throttle, to wake up each morning with my brain ablaze with power that by the end of the day has agreeably run down into fatigue, having propelled my pencil ten pages further into the unknown, and then wake up the next morning and do the same thing over again, day after day, week after week, month after month.

I saw myself, amusingly perhaps, as solving a problem everyone wanted a solution to. What is the meaning, the significance, of this so-various, so-complex world that surrounds us, full of shifting shapes, colors, motions, and sounds? Is it alien from us? An expression of ourselves? Our motions through it, like paddlings of a swimmer in a lake—are they guided by the water or by the swimmer? Why is it we move in one direction or another, in response to what we call our desires? And is it really our desires that propel us from within, or is it the magnetic pull of this world tugging at us from without? What is the meaning of our sense that we must have X or Y? What if we simply decide we need not? What to make of the sheer multifaceted nature of existence?

I thought—now, it seems, touchingly—that if I worked hard enough and turned out to have enough talent, that my works would be welcomed as the Major Contributions to Literature I believed they were, celebrated for their complexity, their virtuosity, and their profundity. People would Understand both them and, perhaps for the first time, me. I assumed that when they were done, things would happen they way they do in the movies: I put the manuscript in the mailbox (shot of the package going in), and wait for the phone call a week later. Okay, two weeks. After all, the only reason major publishers put out the sort of drivel they did, I reasoned, was that they couldn't get enough of the really quality stuff.

It cost me many decades to see the humor in this belief. Now, that seems the most humorous thing of all.

Rive Gauche

I was relentless, just like the young man in "The Alien Corn," I didn't know if I had "it" or not: that's what remained to be seen. Because I was so hard on myself, I despised poseur wannabes in berets on the Left Bank or in the Village, people who spent their time talking about the great things they were going to accomplish rather than shutting up, sitting down, and seeing if they could in fact do them. For that matter, I despised anyone who needed the warmth of others to convince themselves they were living the *Vie de Bohème*. This was being very soft on one's self indeed, and I knew the only way to succeed was to be ruthless. The only way to find out if I could do it, over and over, was to go each day and leave at the end of the afternoon with ten pages in pages hand-written in pencil on a child's lined paper. Each day I proved to myself that I did; doing so again and again assuaged my anxiety. Now I can't hand write a thank-you note longhand without getting muscle cramps in my hand.

I'm amused at academics who write self-important treatises on the Age of Hopkins (Gerard Manley) or the Age of Dickinson (Emily), as if it made sense to label an entire time period with the name of a writer completely unknown during his or her time. Certainly no one in Amherst, much less New York or Paris, would have thought he or she was living in the "Age of Dickinson." Such writers as Dickinson or Hopkins were plucked posthumously from the sea of obscurity that otherwise would have engulfed them. Before they were so plucked, was their time already their Age? Have we no responsibility to try and see the time the way those alive with them saw it? Besides, most people most of the time don't see themselves as living in any Age at all: reality is the taste of dinner, the scraping of the chair along the floor. Who's to say that there are not other similarly un-plucked obscure writers completely irrelevant to their times writing today?

Like the poet Thomas Gray, I now think that the Pantheon of Great Literature, to which I came to believe I belonged as the pencil filled page after page of lined paper, is formed mostly by chance, picking among the people who not only produce works—the minimum requisite—but are at the right place at the right time. Mute inglorious Miltons are simply out of luck. So are non-mute ones who somehow don't get picked up by an agent. We can't pride ourselves that cream rises to the top. We pay attention to the ones we pay attention to. How do we know how many we have failed to be aware of? This is true in a more general sense as well: we're very aware of the things we're aware of, and have to constantly remind ourselves that others need not be so at all.

Of course, the converse isn't true. Being known in your own lifetime doesn't guarantee history's imprimatur. Not everyone who won the Prix de Rome is important. Yet think how thrilled they were! Look at the list of Pulitzer Prize winners for the last century and see how many you recognize. Indeed winning prizes at too early an age may show merely a comfortable talented mediocrity, a facility that others can readily understand.

Still, the future is limited in the slate from which it chooses: it can only anoint those it knows about. Those who didn't win the Prix de Rome, or gain equivalent status somehow, aren't even in the running. Being known is a pre-condition of even being considered. Think of *People Magazine's* annual "100 Most Beautiful People in the World" issue. What it really means is, 100 Most Beautiful Movie Actors (with a few pop stars and sports figures thrown in): you have to be Somebody to be beautiful, it seems. I'd say half the students at any major state university are as nice looking as the faces lionized by *People Magazine*. But they're not Somebody. Isn't it a vicious, or perhaps to those involved in it virtuous, circle, that the fact of attention being paid produces the conviction that these people should be paid attention to?

No more stories

One thing was crystal clear to me. Drama was dead. Or as Gertrude Stein put it, "There are no more stories." Why should we spend all our time, like Madame Bovary, reading about the more exciting exploits of people we would never be? Why should we read about people who do things we'd never want to do? Like dying early deaths, running unwise risks, being subject to physical or mental danger? We do all we can to protect ourselves from these things. Why suddenly should we want to fantasize about doing them? Because our lives are boring? If we need to change our lives, we should do so. Why couldn't literature speak to the real problems of existence, not hype us up with insulin or testosterone jolts of things we would never really ever want to do? Each of us is condemned to live in his or her own body, in his or her own world: the problems of relating to the world around us are, ultimately, the important ones. Reading about others leading more exciting lives only puts off the inevitable fact of having to deal with them.

Besides, the interactions of human beings just aren't that interesting, most of the time: they're so predictable, so banal. 98% of any given conversation, overheard from afar, is completely predictable: we can say with fair certainty what the next person will respond. Or how he or she will feel. But why are feelings important? They're just as transitory and just as predictable as anything else.

I thought nobody wanted to read yet another predictable story about people having an epiphany, or coming to terms with something. The more formulaic genres of heists and murders were of course beneath my notice: dramatic things might happen in them, but they were empty escapes that only made sense for people whose lives weren't like this at all. For the people involved in them, the world was the same as it was for each of us, consisting of the weight of the body, the need for (say) a cup of coffee, the motes in the air, the buzzing of a fly.

The question facing me then became: What would literature look like for people who weren't trying to escape their lives? How could we uncover the lodes of interest right before us, in the here and now?

What I never understood was why everyone wanted the same limited number of things, why people were bent on continuing in the same tired paths of everyone else, say to get a movie star's autograph, or have an object owned by Someone Famous, or Get On A Show—or, in the literary equivalent, go where Famous Writers had gone, do what Famous Writers had done. Why should we configure our world only based on what others wanted us to get out of it, or what they wanted themselves? When we sit in our car at a red light, the traffic island to our side is full of enough details to keep us interested for hours: the overlong grass, the puffballs of dandelions gone to seed, the patching of the asphalt up the side of the white concrete. And yet most of us breeze on by, intent on (say) earning enough money to buy a Designer Something, or going to the "in" restaurant. But once we buy it or eat it, we have it and it is reduced to a series of sensations: flat smooth, colored, dull— or once again we are hungry.

I was entranced by the behinds and backs of public places meant to face a certain direction, like statues that were unfinished on the back, where they stashed the person pulling the strings so that the people out front could "have a good time": the dingy or gun-metal gray back stairwells of otherwise grand hotels, the frying smells and patterned floors in a restaurant kitchen, backstage at the theater. Everything had a back, in this sense: famous people sat down to rest their feet and wiped away the smile, silenced the booming voice. And how would we react to them then?

I noted too the gulf between the drumrolls introducing Experiences we were supposed to get a thrill from, and how we react in fact. Why all this noise for a tiny segment of the world that, like all the other things in life, got old, wore out, and wasn't really much fun? We could look forward for months to event X and, once we found ourselves there, the day finally come, feel only the texture of the seat under us, see the scuffs of someone's shoes, taste the sensations of some food lingering in our mouth, or the hand cream on our lips. And yet we'd probably feel we were responsible for not "having a good time." What I realized was that being primed to expect an Intense Experience was a virtual guarantee that it wouldn't be intense at all. And the converse was true as well: our most vivid experiences invariably took place when we were least expecting them to happen. The aura of the desirable is only in the desiring, not an intrinsic quality of the thing desired. And this meant organizing the details of your life by adopting other people's versions of what we ought to value was inadequate.

How, then, to organize them? In technical terms this meant, How to write literature that wasn't based on a story? In *Twilley*, which I finished in November of that first year in 1974, I was still tied to plot—though very loosely: a young man takes a walk through a department store, goes to the small town where he had grown up, visits with his grandmother (I saw everything, down to the nicks in the wax fruit that she had kept in her back bedroom where the inadequate surface layer of color was chipped away to show the milky white of the wax within), and masturbates in a scene of formless melancholy in a field. This skeleton of a plot became an excuse for me to string sentences with imbedded clause after imbedded clause, with the challenge for me being how long I could keep them aloft before I returned to another detail in the world.

The longest section was a walk through a department store, based on my memories of the old Woodward and Lothrop Department Store in downtown Washington, now long since bankrupt and empty, then a carnival of sights and sounds to the wanderer. The department store was the longest departure from the world in a book consisting largely of departures from the world—embellishments on it, showing the reader that in the meanest flower that blows, or the sight of hanks of hair in different colors hanging on a rack in a department store—we can find more interest than in yet another thriller about The President Being Kidnapped. If we could see the President, we'd find a man with wrinkles. If we could *be* the President, we'd still have to deal with hunger, and the roll around our middle, and people wanting things. Reality always bites you in the ass; why not deal with it head-on? The side of the road was as interesting as a Hollywood Star's house. Only, of course, it wasn't a Hollywood Star's house. In order to get the things you had to give up getting something everybody else wanted; in return you had your fill of things nobody wanted. Hence the scene with masturbation, the ultimate act of aloneness mixed with pleasure, function mixed with functionlessness.

Masturbation

For that matter, all my sex at that time was masturbatory; indeed it now seems that my life was masturbatory, with both the advantages and disadvantages that entails. The advantages are clear: it's a world of fantasy, and always available. You don't have to actually find a partner, or keep that person around. Its disadvantages are equally clear: it lacks the roughness of reality that keeps us paying attention. We can imagine anything. In a sense, we are too free. We're in control, yes: too much so.

Since then, I have gone through periods of intense, unrelenting promiscuity and years of marital fidelity, as well as years of more average unmarried sexuality. These changes of sexual gears convinced me that the way we want to interact with the world, and with other people, determines the way our hormones play out in sex, not the reverse. The same man, full of the same hormones, can during different periods of his life either shun or embrace women as something abhorrent to him or more necessary than food. When I was caught in my youthful writing frenzy, all I was conscious of was the feeling of being pregnant with a god within me, and having to give birth to him. The thought of the distraction of a particular person, of being once again tied to the minutiae of the world though interaction, was horrible to me. And then there have been times where the only time I felt real was pounding into a woman.

The Prussian war theorist Carl von Clausewitz is often quoted as saying that "War is a continuation of politics (policy: the German word is "Politik") by other means." Sometimes this is taken as a wake-up call to the professional military: war isn't its own end, it's a part of a larger constellation of acts that states undertake to achieve their goals. In the same way, sex is an expression of our relationship with the world. What we do sexually is determined by what our relation is. Most men have a "type" of women they are attracted to, and a sort of sex they typically like to have with them. The trick is, figuring out what these things are. Nobody is born knowing whether he wants to dominate smaller women, or be dominated by more assertive ones. So too for someone whose type in women is leggy blondes: maybe he just hasn't met the petite brunette he'd kill for. The same thing must be true of other sexual partner categories. Though Keith, I believe, was 100% gay, I am still not convinced that sexual orientation is innate. It can be absolute without being innate; all this means is that he never changed enough to change his relationship with the world. But in theory, he could have done so.

Conservatives frequently insist that homosexuality is a "choice." This seems to me to be true to the extent that by using the word "choice" we mean that our sexual objects are mutable, the opposite of "fixed forever." Yet (and this is the problem with the right wing's position) all too frequently it is taken to mean we can accept or decline something at will: that we are somehow external to the choosing process. Instead, it's pretty clear that when we desire, whoever or whatever it is we desire, the vector arrow drives us forward and won't let us do otherwise. That arrow can change direction. This doesn't mean, we can make it change direction. A man whose adult "type" is petite, simpering women who tells himself that tomorrow he's going to desire vixens is unlikely to achieve his goal. Nor is it likely he can be forced or tortured through electro-shock therapy into doing so. But it's not out of the question that some day this may become his preferred type, if his life changes to make that possible. How, at any rate, can this statement ever be disproved? It's just that most people's adult lives, once fixed, don't change much. And of course, the only way we would be able to say that his life had changed was by seeing that his sexual "type" had changed as well.

Clever

My tastes in literature have changed utterly since those days of glory in the flower. Books are like sexual objects: when we want them, we really want them. But thinking they have any objective power to move us is an error. At that point, I loved language with the energy of a racehorse let out of the gate constructed by everyday speech. Proust, whose vast masterwork I had read the summer before my last year of college, beginning in French but switching to English after a book or two as I realized I wasn't keeping to my schedule, could not have sentences long enough for me—all those beautiful imbedded clauses, strung out across the page, the fact that occasionally he'd drop one. Nabokov. *Gravity's Rainbow.* Wodehouse—of course. Bertie, Aunt Dahlia, Gussie Fink-Nottle, Honoria Glossop, Jeeves. The mere invocation of their names makes me smile now—and Wodehouse is the only one of my fetish writers of early youth I can still read with any pleasure. It's so overtly trivial it works: Nabokov has long since become tiresome, my then-favorite novel, *Ada*, having sat on the shelf unread for decades. Could I read *Gravity's Rainbow* ever again? Now I'm simply exasperated with "clever" prose writers, as with most poetry savoring its own words: life is too short, and the "look at me" aspect of sparkling language simply seems immature. (Yet they are, it seems, what sell as well as any "serious literature" sells.)

Thus, I found banal the great academic debate of the 1990s, the so-called "canon wars," with the radicals fighting the conservatives to see which books would end up on the syllabus. It was like the scholar's version of Flaubert's famous dictum that "all life existed to end up in a book." Was all life destined to end up as part of a curriculum? How silly. Ultimately it didn't matter what got put on the syllabus and what not, given the immensely greater personal variations with respect to each work than between any two works. You couldn't assure that the black students would like works by black authors the best; fighting as if it mattered over what got taught had to assume that reactions to works could be predicted.

So much contemporary art is tiresome for the same reasons—all those works where we're supposed to admire the surface of the canvas, or the texture of the jute, or the wittiness of the experience we get if we devote our entire attention to this object alone. The world is full of so many more interesting things, all to be got for nothing, and just by looking. Such as: the slope of unmown hay caught in the late afternoon sun, soft-looking from a distance; the clouds of trees hovering over the top of the house like the world's packing material, the shining puddle of mercury-colored sealant that has run into round-edge shapes in the center of the road after the insertion of reflective brackets in the road's broken line, like congealed blood the same color but not consistency as the wounds in the roads. Why should I drive all the way into Washington and stare fixedly at a small object on the wall that won't even be comparably interesting rather than merely taking a walk? Of course that's what the artist wants me to do, because he or she wants to feel he or she is in control of the world. But nobody controls the world, it makes boats bobble about on its surface, with us asserting vainly and somewhat touchingly that we do in fact exercise "command of the seas."

The day after I finished *Twilley* I began another work. I called it *Whaley;* both names were family names local to the Eastern Shore. I'm sure it will never be published, because here I left the pretense of any plot whatever, an external structure, and allowed one set of details to generate others, instead of coming back after flights away from the world to other things in the same scene. It was important for me to see that I could in fact get lost in the woods: there was no particular point in returning to the common world. The fact that getting lost worked as well as remaining, even if vestigially, in the common world, showed us that we need not be bound by the demands of others. Why should others hang around to be told off?

This brought up a new problem. If I rejected structuring based on stories that told the same lies over and over—that Who Shot the President was more interesting than Who Shot the Neighbor—how could I deal with the fact of other people? If I rejected the hierarchy, with brand names higher than non-brand names, and the pernicious lie that what you spend lots of money for was by definition a better experience than what you didn't as well as the lie that reading about the changes to a small finite number of people *mattered* in the larger scheme of things, how was I ever to structure? These were, after all, apparently the presuppositions of the vast majority of the human race. Lack of structure in a sense solved the problem, showing that the world was based on a vast lode of unstructured material. But one lack of structure is very much like another. I couldn't do it twice.

Dance boom

I found my answer in dance—more specifically in the works of George Balanchine. In the mid-1970s the "dance boom" had just begun, and indeed all the arts were flourishing, not least of all in Washington, drunk on the possibilities inherent in its first world-class set of performing halls. American Ballet Theatre, New York City Ballet, the Metropolitan Opera, Vienna Opera, and countless others streamed in and out.

Keith played the 'cello in the Kennedy Center Opera House orchestra, and I tagged along. Back then they allowed hangers-on, such as me, simply to stand in the orchestra pit. Finally all that was stopped by the management, but by that time, I was gone from Washington. I would stand with my back to the dull-black-painted curve of the orchestra pit wall right by the first violins, or more usually back by the double basses, motionless, only a few feet from the greatest dancers and singers in the world. When the pit was too full to accommodate me, the kindly head usher would find a seat in the house row out front.

In this way I continued an arts education that had begun when my mother took Keith and me to matinée performances of the National Ballet of Washington (she and I had our pictures in *Life* magazine with Edward Villella after being taken backstage by a friend of hers who was at the time the Ballet's general manager; I remember going to the drug store in Salisbury to buy some copies, and wanting to show the check-out girl: look! I'm in *Life* magazine!) and continued with New York City Ballet at Saratoga.

I saw Baryshnikov's first Western appearance, with American Ballet Theatre, when the crowd screamed and screamed (he did solos), an amazing impersonation of a human pretzel by Allegra Kent in Balanchine's *Agon*, and a riveting performance by the ill-fated Gelsey Kirkland in Anthony Tudor's *The Lilac Garden*. This opened with a tableau of her leaning against her lover; the thing was, her bosom was heaving as the curtain rose, expressing the unseen argument into which we have been plunged. *Agon* was on the same program with Jerome Robbins' masterpiece of perversion, *The Cage*, where a swarm of wild-haired females tear out the viscera of a hapless male ("it's just the second act of *Giselle*," Robbins is supposed to have said in his defense), and with the closest-thing-to-a-Balanchine-X-rated-ballet, *Bugaku*, where the Japanese bridegroom deflowers the bride in a ritual mating that would have caused octopi to be envious.

Week after week, while I was pouring out my youthful works by day, I saw masterpiece after masterpiece at night merely by getting in the car with Keith. At the same time, I got to feel like a part of the show, if for no other reason than that I ran around downstairs. Baryshnikov and I crossed in the maze of corridors under the stage; I remember thinking how short he was. Mr. Balanchine, the last living Modernist genius, Stravinsky and Picasso being dead, and the century's greatest choreographer, gallantly held the door for me one evening as I rushed heedlessly down the stairs on the way to somewhere unimportant. (My mother's longer encounter with Mr. B, as the dancers called him, took place in the Grand Union in Saratoga Springs over the cabbages, where they discussed Melissa Hayden's farewell performance of the night before.) It was heady stuff for a twenty-year-old: at the time I took it for granted, unaware that it was an amazing time in a golden era, and one that I was getting under the very best of circumstances, with no particular energy investment on my part.

I think Keith liked having me along, though he never said so. The fact that we had something to do made it possible for us just to be with each other, with no attempt at any greater verbal intimacy. Probably these countless evenings together while he went about his business and while I worshiped at the shrine of Art were the only way we could have interacted during those years, given how difficult he was, and given my immersion in an internal world. I took my naps on the big sofas downstairs in the musicians' lounge, ate in the performers' cafeteria, and was very happy.

It may be that this period seems so beautiful, so luminous, precisely because Keith is dead, I am no longer twenty years old and drunk on the illusion of limitless possibilities, and the culture boom of the early 70s is over, with Mr. B in his grave for more than twenty years. Is it Keith I miss? Or merely a time in my own life? When you're young, it's "very heaven to be alive," as Wordsworth put it—because you haven't figured out that what you want isn't possible. Envy the ignorant.

I thought the answer to the problem I found after *Whaley* was Balanchine, or at least a version of Balanchine for literature. Balanchine had rejected plot in favor of, early on, fragments of plot (as in *Serenade*) and then made works with no plot at all, structuring his works according to the external skeletons of works of music, and made the motions and interactions between the dancers the point ("the minute you put a man and a woman on the stage together, you have a drama"). And whole rooms-full of people came to see, to applaud, and to understand. If it worked for him, why not for me? So what if I was an unknown 20-year-old and he one of the great Modernist geniuses? This kind of realization surely came to him in just the same way, and felt the same to him, as it did to me. I had no warning signs that there were things I couldn't do: all was possible, if I remained pure, worked hard, and didn't give in to distractions. Above all, if I went about my business as anonymously as possible. For if I let on what I was doing, someone was sure to want me to do X, Y, and Z—given that others want us to do things they can understand at sight and recognize as a known commodity, not things we are in the process of defining. All art and thought would have been nipped in the bud had others been able to see it before it was finished. They would have filled the time with a thousand things that seemed more substantial.

Structure Opera

My own *Apollo* was a book I now call, after Gertrude Stein's unsuccessful-but-interesting "operas" in words, *A Structure Opera*. For what I had realized is that structure is all around us, waiting to be utilized.

Structure can be found in anything: in the patterns of an analog watch face, for example. Clearly the quarter hours are less interesting visually than something drooping gracefully to the right with the longer leg being drawn towards 6, say 1:26 or so, or perhaps 2:22. 12:00 is quite uninteresting, as is 6:00: they're far too regular. The watch dial has boring points, settings we find banal and uninteresting precisely because they are so seminal to our use of the thing—like most of the world. Using a hammer to hit nails, at least normal nails, at least the usual number, at least for usual construction, can't be art. But merely avoiding the obvious doesn't, conversely, mean the result is art. Without looking at it, we can't say whether it'll be an interesting avoidance of the boring or just meaningless: most of the world, after all, is off the track of these so-well-known-they're-boring things.

Making art requires having us identify the things that are banal, and then skewing what we do slightly to the side. Too far away and we cannot sense a relationship between what is done and what isn't. Too close and they become banal. Sometimes we express these banal things as "functional," so that it seems art is part of an absolute duality of functionality on one hand, art on the other. But 2:22 isn't less functional than 12:00. It's just not banal. Much functionality *is* banal for various reasons. But it's not banal merely because it's functional.

In *A Structure Opera*, I went on an orgy of structuring, finding the strong magnet points that had to be avoided in many things: patterns of letters (some hang below the line and some tower above it, some are round and some are linear, so that bbbbbbbbb is nothing but boring, as is bpbpbpbpbpb, but—to add a letter— bplppbbbqllqqqblllbbpqb isn't; neither is bbpbbpppppbbbpb), number series (1-3-5- 7-9 from a line-up of numbers from 1 to 10 is boring but 1-6-7 isn't, even if it's somewhat minimalistic), even things as abstruse as arrangements of photocopies taken at varying distances from the glass, ranging from close up to far away (the photographs were Hill and Adamson calotypes, intrinsically interesting) or choreography for chess pieces, abstract "games."

Each day brought new discoveries: the whole world, I realized in a rush of adrenaline, could be structured. I realized along the way that some of the simpler structures in the world weren't interesting in their own right, but rather as examples of my point, that structuring was possible. The point in *A Structure Opera* was their ubiquity, hitherto (it seemed to me) overlooked by people living to get a glimpse of a Movie Star on celluloid or (gasp) in the flesh as a way of structuring their lives. I was going to show them how to liberate themselves from the chains of collective desire, show them that the world was full of things available to them, and that they need not spend their time running fruitlessly after things they would never, by definition, attain. What I failed to realize was that they liked the chase.

A Structure Opera was Book #3. Book #4 during those glory years was a series of parables of the creative process with footnotes that gradually took over as bearers of the parables. I saw myself as documenting my creative process for posterity that would, of course, be interested in everything. I got this idea by seeing that posterity does pore even over the marginalia of some people. Thus I concluded: when the light of attention is trained on us, everything we do is interesting. I had merely got the causality wrong, not realizing that it is the training of the light of attention that makes things interesting, not that things are interesting and so are noticed. We can't, in fact, pull ourselves up by our own bootstraps. (I realized this later when editors told me that memoirs had to be by people who were already famous.)

Lost in this esoteric world, I nonetheless took out the trash, went to the grocery store, cooked dinner, cleaned up, said "hi" to the pleasant elderly lady who lived upstairs, and drove each day to the library, where I melted into the crowd of scruffy students. Who would have known that from looking at me?

Unhappy arrangement

In these years after college, I got what I think of as my second B.A. I took my own course in film at the now long-since demolished Circle Theater on Pennsylvania Avenue. Every two to three days the double feature changed. I went three times a week, sitting in darkness to see double features of all the European classics (Bergman, Fellini) and the American movies of a couple of years before, from what now seems the golden age of the 1970s. I read voraciously: Gertrude Stein seemed to me so logical as if I had invented it in a dream myself and then forgotten, Virginia Woolf what I would have been myself if I had been a woman given to nervous depression rather than a man who (at the time) thought he was invincible. Modernism was my language.

I had budgeted a year for *Twilley*. I finished it in November, and found someone on campus to begin typing it, all 600 pages, typed from the pencil manuscript on lined paper. It was an unhappy arrangement, with the typist's version full of mistakes that only the author could have corrected, as well as bereft of the last-minute fixes that are a fact of the writing life. So after a few hundred pages, I took over myself. In typing it, I was as much a man possessed as I had been in writing it, convinced somehow that only this translation to the taps of a machine stood between me and history. I would continue to type even when Keith had visitors over; my place was secure as the eccentric little brother. And of course this was before computers, so that every mistake had to be manually corrected, and the whole re-read for errors. The manuscript was covered with pen marks and spots of white correction fluid.

I sent off *Twilley* thinking I had fulfilled my bargain with the world: I had worked hard, been pure, produced. Now I was ready to reap my reward. The most horrifying, puzzling period of my life began when the manuscript came back to me for the first time, pasted over with the postage stamps that I had enclosed for just that purpose. Then it happened again. And again, and again. Sometimes it returned with letters expressing disbelief that I had wasted time on such nonsense, but more often it boomeranged with printed rejection slips. This was more than 30 years ago. Nowadays, I'd get a printed slip the next day saying that nothing could be considered without an agent.

Naif that I was, I was devastated by this rejection, as I was devastated by the rejection of the books that followed. Writing these things was like breathing to me. Worse, I thought this is what the world wanted me to do. I had something to say; I had said it. I had sacrificed and remained pure. Now, it was beginning to be clear, no one was remotely interested. Hard work? Who cared? Purity? Ridiculous! I felt like an actor finishing a performance of *Hamlet*, thinking he had never been better, never more focused and on-key, who suddenly realizes that the audience he had imagined in the theater was non-existent, the rows of empathetic spectators only empty chairs. What, he might wonder, was that all about? Why all these countless days pushing back the border of the unknown? To what purpose the self-imposed discipline? To what purpose the meals, the sleep, the trips to the store, all in the service of this pencil unraveling its interrupted thread across lined pages? What implications from the fact that their quality and value was so clear to me and denied in such a unified chorus by everyone else? Was I crazy?

I know what it is to have touched absolute bottom, to sit motionless in a chair from morning to night, watching the sun rise and then set, punctuated only by food and trips to the bathroom. This was the only period of my life when I ever contemplated suicide, however briefly. The problem, I realized, was that any suicide we can effect in suburbia leaves the body, a hunk of useless meat that others must deal with. This I was unwilling to do to anyone. If there had been a way to vaporize, I would have gladly vaporized. I now know that even without a body to dispose of, suicide ineluctably marks those who must deal with it: I think of the heavy cost many people paid for the suicide of Tom Goldberg (as he might well have been named), Martha's first husband, including both Martha and myself: it is the ultimately aggressive, most absolutely selfish act. Is this why the Church considers it is a sin? Still, I think that everybody should know what it feels like when the impetus forward that is the sign of healthy life simply grinds to an utter halt. Point zero, the absolute inertia of stillness. Having felt the motion most of us take for granted in this manner (Heidegger's *Geworfenheit*, I later thought) falter and fail, I was forever made grateful for normalcy, and for the energy that so many people are not even conscious of.

This period also made me realize, as the period before it had not been able to do, that people can be caught in life-patterns with trajectories either up or down, that they have no choice but to follow. Just as I had no choice but to follow the path upwards, now I had to walk into the valley. I don't have much patience with people who assert that everything can be achieved by those who try, that being "motivated" is the sufficient condition for success. It may not even be a necessary condition, and it certainly isn't a sufficient one. I could no sooner have "snapped out of" my depression during my journey through the valley of despair than I could have snapped out of my exhilaration during the time when I was flying high on the belief in my own capabilities. By the same token, when the period is over, it's over. There's no point asking someone while he or she is going through such a period if it will ever end: the person won't know. All we can do is note the fact that we are taken by the scruff of the neck in this fashion and whirled away for a ride.

One sign of my condition during my time in the valley of the shadow was that I saw a film of the Polish director Andrej Wajda called *Ashes and Diamonds*, and fell in love with it: for years, I thought it was the greatest film ever made. (I saw it decades later and realized from my indifference I was no longer that person.) Set in the waning days of the Resistance in Warsaw, it tells the story of a young freedom fighter, with whom I identified horribly, who falls in love with a beautiful young woman and has a one-night stand. Later that night he is killed: a bit of happiness, a few diamonds, in a world otherwise of ashes. To me, it symbolized existence. I took to smoking strong cigarettes like him for a brief period, perhaps as much as a week, in homage. I can still re-create the jolt as the nicotine-laden smoke hit my lungs.

At my nadir, in 1976, the third year after I had graduated from college, I got a job as a lowly *surveillant*, or proctor, at the French *Lyçée* in Washington. It was like forcing myself to move forward when all I wanted to do was collapse and die. Still I must have had enough of the life force left to realize I had to do something. At the French School I took attendance, monitored classes whose teachers were absent, and sat in a cramped office with the other *surveillant*, an affable if uneducated young French woman married to a Texan. But at least my radically-underpaid job (my salary was $7500, I remember, which even in 1976 was peanuts, and not very many of them) moved my body out of the apartment every morning and brought it back every night. I did my daily run, fixed food, was affable with my colleague and interacted with the students. My colloquial French improved exponentially.

Part of my duties as a *surveillant* was to ride the school bus every evening with the children to make sure they didn't stick out of windows. The end of the run was the Watergate Office Building, where the bus driver and I, a friendly no-pretensions guy in his late 20s named Greg, would park the bus with the flashers on and go down to the Watergate Pastry Shop for Viennese pastries. Then we'd get back to the school in Bethesda just in time for me to hit the worst part of Beltway gridlock. I was a robot moving through its motions.

Mr. Average

So many of my relationships with other people during this time were transitory, secondary (Keith's friends), or indirect—even with Keith, the person I spent the most time with. Indeed, my most direct relationship with him was through a book. One day in 1974 or 75 Keith came home carrying a magazine that turned out to be the *National Lampoon High School Yearbook Parody*. Over the next years, we spent countless hours with this increasingly well-thumbed object, memorizing practically every word and screaming with laughter until tears rolled down our cheeks.

The Yearbook, as we came to call it in fond abbreviation and acknowledgment of one-and-onlyness, was ostensibly a copy of a yearbook from C. Estes Kefauver High School (Adlai Stevenson's running mate, and so for the people at the Lampoon, synonymous with 50s and with loser) in the town of "Dacron" (= 50s, boring) Ohio. What we held in our hands was supposed to be the particular copy belonging to a Mr. Average named Larry Kroger. All the names in the book were paranomastic, names that mimic phrases, or had dumb associations. Kroger is a grocery store chain popular in the Midwest and South; the music teacher was "Dwight Mannesburden" (make the first name bi-syllabic); the Spanish teacher "Dolores Panatella." Through the "handwritten" comments by various class members on the pages, the reader pieces together the relationships between the school's constellation of cheerleaders, class politicians, "beatniks," tough girls, and girl-who-gets-pregnant constituting this fictional but achingly typical small-town American high school.

Most of all, we learn about Mr. Average himself, Larry Kroger. By following the information artfully included in the "writing" of the his classmates, we learn that he has the hots for one of the prom queen types ("Fridge"), who won't give him the time of day, and in turn is pursued by the peppy short girl who supports all teams and draws circles over her "i"s and drives a car named "Mr. Beep-Beep." His embarrassingly average English tests are enclosed as if bundled together in a pile with the year book, as are his embarrassingly average school records ("may not be college material"—this in the first or second grade), and his embarrassingly average graffiti.

The book was funny because it was filled with hilarious throw-away jokes, causing us to explode as we made the connections so lovingly embedded in the material by the writers, such as the fact that Larry had clearly asked Fridge to the prom months and months before the fact and had been turned down for reasons variously reported by her girlfriends ("she really had to wash her hair that night"). But its profundity came from the fact that it makes clear the utterly typal nature of all such seemingly individual worlds, C. Estes Kefauver High School, or by extension my high school, not therefore a be-all and end-all world-in-itself, but only one single instantiation among countless others of a peculiarly American institution. This was hardly news to us, but we were nonetheless delighted to have it so publicly acknowledged.

The surest way to refute the claims to piety and obedience leveled so absolutely on their subjects by all the petty monarchies known as small-town American high schools was simply to show that, in the larger scheme of things, they were all in fact nothing but *pays d'operette*, ridiculous and pretentious. How liberating it was for Keith and me to think that people we had never met had also hated the chains and shackles of a world that everyone around them asserted was absolute reality, understanding like us that what others took for reality was in fact only the shadow of a shadow, dust in the wind, good only for ridicule and laughter.

Martha and I, then married, went back to our high school for our twentieth class reunion. I had not been back since graduation, though she had gone to her tenth reunion, with Tom. (If she had wanted, she could have gone to her thirtieth reunion with husband #3—and indeed may have done so). I visited Martha and Tom shortly before this, and remember then thinking how pitiful Tom was, learning names and memorizing Martha's stories of "he was the one who . . ." from Martha's copy of the (very real) High School Yearbook so he would know whom he was meeting, as if trying precisely to acquire a feel for the small- town clubbiness I had found so stultifying. It seemed to me he wanted to put on instant small-town history to fill a void created by the Bronx High School of Science, like someone from *Blade Runner* with a head full of artificial memories.

Martha and I wanted especially to go to our high school reunion, as I recall, to show off the unlikelihood of our marriage. High school in fact has had the last laugh, if it wanted to have it: this so-unlikely pairing in fact turned out to be untenable, and probably that for many of the reasons that it would have been thought unlikely to begin with. At any rate, we went. What I found on arrival was that there was no longer a dragon to slay. It had died long ago, and the reality it had left behind was only dull and at most, rather pitiful. Only when transmuted to the gold of *The Yearbook* could high school still hold my interest. Or was it *The Yearbook* that had slain the dragon through laughter?

Those few moments of closeness to Keith during this period when we laughed ourselves sick over *The Yearbook* were augmented by others; indeed this is the period past high school when we were the closest. Keith was getting a Ph.D. at Catholic University, writing a dissertation on Gregorian Chant. He was, I believe, still a virgin, and undoubtedly remained so until, when I was away at the University of Chicago several years later, he met Michael.

Midway

The logical end of this series of early books came during an unhappy year in Chicago, where, realizing finally I had no alternative to further education, I went after the *Lyçée*. I could, I realized one day, running along the Midway and feeling wretched, take fragments of life ripped whole from the flesh of the world, and arrange them. Sometimes all the stars are in alignment: we go outside in the morning and see the dew on the grass, glinting in the sun, the damp globes of the silvered dandelions, a gray board thrown aside that catches the sun, and a trailing string dropped the day before. It all seems to make sense, seems like the production of a coherent sensibility—before falling apart a moment later.

If any single element in such configurations had been absent, there would be no coherence: without the dew, no glinting, without the board, no connection between the dandelions and the string, without the string no curve on the ground to match that of the dandelion globes. And in an instant, all this can alter, or with the raising of the sun a few more degrees—much like Cartier-Bresson's perfect moments, caught by the camera lens and forced to stay: the man jumping over the puddle at just this point, the Indian woman swaying just this amount to the left, the portly Hitchcock-esque man walking by the pattern of holes at just this moment.

It wasn't enough, then, to see that the world was shot through with the possibility of structure. I had to arrange the perfect moments, things that were vastly more interesting in themselves than mere numbers or letters or even watch faces. The result was my first work completely free of plot, Book #5. I called it *Fragments in the Form of a Calendar*. Starting with a list of months, flowers, and birthstones, I strung together a group of such configurations, things I had stumbled across in my life or remembered. The world was all around us, vastly more complex than our wildest dreams, if we could only become aware of it.

I wasn't giving meaning to the world, only documenting it. I had, I thought, solved the problem of the Russian Formalists, who thought that average people had to pass through the artist to perceive the world. Victor Shklovsky for example, insisted that only "art makes the stone stoney." Without art, he thought, people couldn't perceive their own lives. Such a view was only possible so close to Romanticism, with its exaggerated claims for the importance of the artist. Romanticism, in unadulterated form, was clearly dead. It was clear that in the 1970s in the blue-collar suburbs where I lived that the artist wasn't, as Victor Hugo called him, a Magus (singular of Magi), a wise man leading the way to wisdom. Neither was he Baudelaire's albatross, soaring above the mariners who ultimately brought him down and mocked him. But he could at least show people that they had overlooked the most important thing of all, free them from their useless, fruitless crush to See a Movie Star or read fantasies about The World Taken Over By A Madman.

This period of my life ended with *Fragments*. During my year at Chicago, I made myself and my professors miserable by defining just how far every author I had to read was from the vision I had defined for myself—just, that is, how much each was deficient in not being Bruce Fleming. Not that even I thought the works of Bruce Fleming were better than the works of, say, Chaucer or Rabelais, but that they exactly filled the comparably-shaped hole in Bruce Fleming in a way that Rabelais and Chaucer did not. The professors didn't know what I had written, and of course I didn't tell them. They must have found me strange indeed. I was so agitated in one class that ultimately the professor asked me to stop coming in exchange for my A. I left Chicago after a year with no regrets, and spent a year and a half going to the theater and cinemas in Munich, where I was ostensibly a student at the university in a country where students don't have to go to class.

In Munich I wrote very little. Even I, self-motivated as I was, could only continue for so long in the face of a world uninterested in my existence. The gulf between my vision of myself (an Important Writer) and how the world saw me (an aging student in a world of students) was simply too great, so that I was in danger of falling into this gulf if I thought about it. I would have to swallow this life, forget that I had ever done it—much as (I imagined) Rimbaud forgot that he had ever written the *Illuminations* as a businessman in Africa. And so, for a time, I did.

When I returned from Munich, I found a graduate school that would pay me to get a Ph.D. I knew that for some people that getting a graduate degree was a goal in and of itself. Why not for me? So I got a Ph.D., spent the following summer in Siena on one fellowship and the next year in Berlin on another.

Three
WOMEN, AND BERLIN

Mutability

Part of my youthful work of self-discovery was seeing how much of myself was mutable and how much merely the result of situations. None of us, after all, knows this from the beginning: Keith had to discover who he was sexually—for him that was, I believe, determinative. My sexuality was much closer to home, but I had to displace myself in other ways. For me it was through playing a sort of game with other cultures. I threw myself into them, trying to see if I could melt into them: eat their food, speak their language, think in the terms of their worlds, wear their clothes, "pass" for a native. This worked through Western Europe and even to a degree Eastern Europe, but faltered in Africa. But that is what I'd been aiming at all along: to be bested. All it meant was, I had cut through the transitory layers and finally found what would not change.

So much cant in the 1990s was expended on the Otherness of Other cultures: the claim that we were condemned to see Other cultures as Other, and that we should immediately and fulsomely praise this Otherness, as a contrast to the way our forefathers had denigrated them. The question nobody asked was this: Are they Other at all? I could only find out by seeing if I could fit into them. If I could, they weren't Other. If I couldn't, they were.

Italy was my first stop. The summer I graduated from high school, I spent two months in Rome as a member of a student orchestra. Rome is where I turned 17. Much of our time was taken up practicing, we were policed as a group by the adults, and we lived a bit outside the center, out to the west of Vatican City, so that getting across the Tiber took some doing on several busses and was only feasible on Sundays. Still, my room in the Villa Aurelia was huge and high-ceilinged room, white-walled with windows on both sides from which I had a fabulous view of the Roman pines in the gardens and of the blue blue sky. And so many tiny details were quite different than what I was used to that the fabric of everyday life was a source of constant delight. There was the food that we were served in the equally high-ceilinged dining room: soups vaguely greasy with olive oil, different-tasting meats, and hollow Roman rolls whose tops separate into five separate circles around a center. In the city, there was a street fair, where I thought myself naughty for buying rubbery anis-cookies of women with three breasts, their nipples nicely toasted. There were the used books in stalls on Sundays outside the Stazione Termini. There was the service at St. Peter's, up in front of Bernini's sunburst and

Holy Ghost that my best friend from the orchestra, female—one of those "older women" college students—and I went to. The guard was about to stop her for her skirt being too short, then was himself stopped by his colleague: clearly she was pious, as she was wearing a mantilla over her head. Standing over to the side of Michelangelo's "Pietà" to get out of the way of tourists and merely looking for ten minutes, trying to fix it in my mind; the caricole staircase of the Vatican museums; the day trip to Florence and finding myself *really there*: Ah yes, people always remember the first time.

Now I smile tolerantly at my teen-aged self. What was I thinking to come home with Italian translations of Wodehouse and Byron? The oval labels of the Orangina-like soft drinks? The funny Birra Peroni claw bottle openers we got from bars? I have these still, I think, in the bottoms of drawers. Or have they been thrown out in one of numerous moves? Why was I so taken with *Topolino* (Donald Duck) comic books? The translation of *Uncle Tom's Cabin* into Italian? But I know what I was thinking. Every discovery of an equivalent, or of the thing that functioned like something I was used to, proved that life could be lived in Italian, and by extension in Italy. I could certainly be taken physically for a tall Northern Italian. This was charming, but it was not, I was slowly learning, Other. Many people return again and again to, say, Provence, or Tuscany, as thrilled as ever time and again by the taste of the unsalted Tuscan bread, the lines of trees between the farms, the local wine. Yet such places continue to be charming as places only for those who never accept them as part of themselves.

Gertrude Stein continued all her life to be so taken by Paris, I am sure, only because her French remained so bad. For the people who live there, what foreigners find so charming is banal. For them, the fabric of life itself—all those things that seemed so devastatingly charming to me in Rome, from the sugar dusting on the dolce one paid for in advance in the cafés to the Orangina to the sounds made in the close-walled streets by the Vespa motorscooters—is a means to an end, not the foreground. It all fades into the background, becoming only the stage set for their particular goals and obligations. The natural endpoint when we go somewhere exotic is thus taking that place for granted as the locals take it for granted. Then and only then are we at home. But at that point, there's no more reason to be there than elsewhere.

I have used up the exotic in enough places—having in my turn learned Italian, French, German and Spanish well enough to assimilate, if only temporarily, in each of those cultures—that I no longer seek the exotic. I travel, and momentarily taste a faint version of my youthful conviction that I had entered a fundamentally different world. But I know that this sense is a result of my relationship to this world, not a quality of the world itself, and that every day I spend in the world that initially seems different dilutes the sense of Otherness more and more. In this, travel is like life itself: each day is, in the words of *Romeo and Juliet*'s Friar Lawrence, a day closer to our graves. With travel, each day is a day closer to the point where we no longer taste the exotic, and the Outside world seems fundamentally like the Inside. And when we reach that point, why travel? When we eat the exotic, we're using up a finite resource.

The summer after my first year of college I went to an NYU-run summer school in Paris, where I was completely on my own. I lived in the Maison du Japon (why had NYU contracted with them?) in the Cité Universitaire and took the métro everywhere—to classes, to museums, to the Marais, to Montmartre, to Montparnasse. For several decades after this summer I could still get quite weak-kneed at the smell of the Paris métro, returning from Africa to a friend's borrowed apartment every three months, or visiting friends at other times. Now this smell has all but disappeared, being, I believe, the result of some now-outmoded braking system. In any case, I am no longer thrilled merely to think that part of my life is set in Paris. Part of my life is set in lots of places. Who's keeping score any more? Not even me. It's like thinking you owe the world the preservation of everything you say, as if words were gold spun from nothing. Instead, they're a means to get along, something the living creature needs to get from moment to moment. They die when we die.

I turned 18 that summer in Paris. It was a heady feeling to be on my own, a continual series of challenges to be met. What interesting place would I go today after my classes? This weekend, perhaps to the Marché au Puces at the Porte de Clingancourt? Would I take a ride on the Canal St. Martin east of the Place de la République? Walk yet again in the Luxembourg Gardens? Visit the Jeu de Paume, then the Impressioinist Museum? The museum of the Organgerie, with the Monet Waterlilies? Go to the Comédie Française? Take the train out to Chartes? That was the summer I read Henry Adams and sought The Religious. I didn't find it, exactly, but it was fun being on the trail. The closest I came was a week I spent in Normandy, visiting the Mont Saint-Michel and trying to feel what Adams had felt. Still, I did grow quite maudlin in the American war cemeteries in Normandy, living upstairs in the little inn with the rickety table that all looked like something out of a Van Gogh.

Latin
Living, albeit briefly, in the Latin cities of Rome and Paris liberated me to a degree from the physical repression engendered by high school. A soccer field in Chillum Heights several years later did a great deal more, the weight room some more, energetic and glorious promiscuity yet more, and becoming a model even more. I've made my peace with others.

High school implanted in me the only male beauty ideal available at the time in small-town American high schools. Namely, football players: I didn't want to be a beanpole. Yet in Paris and Rome I saw tall thin men not unlike myself who were apparently considered good-looking, and in any case were quite comfortable showing off their bodies. They wore tight pants that showed the bulge in their crotch, shirts unbuttoned to expose their chest hair and, occasionally, gold chains. My instinctive sense that physicality, and by extension sexuality, was something one didn't flaunt in public, made me feel slightly embarrassed for them. Weren't they supposed to be covering up? Puzzlingly, though, they didn't look or act as if they thought sex was dirty and furtive: they openly made comments to the women, some of whom seemed to enjoy the banter, and talked on the street about women who passed by. Sex, it seemed, was a great game to them, a commonly-enjoyed pastime, a joke adults were in on. It was something people could laugh over rather than deny.

Gee, others might say. So what else is new? Yet the things we discover ourselves at such cost only seem so self-evident to us when we've discovered them. They're true, and it doesn't seem possible we didn't always know them. But we still had to discover them. We all go step by step. And then it's up to the next person to make the same discoveries, and so for each person, over and over, over and over.

The assimilation in Paris and Rome had worked amazingly well. My next try was in Munich. I had been so miserable in Chicago I left vowing I would never again be on the receiving end of formal education—though of course I had left Haverford vowing the same thing—and decided to see if I could be a German, or more precisely, a Bavarian. That worked well for a time too: I sat in the square before the University buildings in Munich stretched out reading little yellow Reclam books, mostly nineteenth-century German classics like Goethe and Shiller, that cost 1 Mark 10 Pfennige per unit (most were tiny things and hence one unit; longer books could be two three or even up to five units, such as the *Kritik der Reinen Vernunft*). I spent countless afternoons in the Lenbachhaus, looking at the whirling Kandinskys exploding from their gray frames set against gray walls. I went to a performance of Chekhov's *Three Sisters* in the Residenztheater that seemed as if it were speaking from my soul. Even though I was in Munich I would never get, at least metaphorically speaking, to Moscow—no one ever does. I went down to the Starnberger See on the weekends with friends. I sat in Irish pubs in Schwabing. I ran in the English Garden. I spoke German well enough that people assumed I was German. Apparently I could "pass" here too. I was 25.

Yet by the time I left Munich I was heartily sick of blue/white, Bavarian accents, women in green coats trailing sausage dogs, and King Ludwig II. The place I'd liked the best in the Germany I saw was cosmopolitan Berlin, where the West German government took foreign students for week-long orientation tours for free in an effort to drum up a little propaganda for the island of West Berlin. It was therefore back to Berlin that I went after my Ph.D. (two years flat in so-nowhere-it's-somewhere Nashville; added up as academic terms, I managed to go from high school to Ph.D. in a total of six years); I spent the summer studying Italian at the University of Siena and at its end took the train north through the Brenner Pass to start my Fulbright in Berlin. There I continued the game of displacement: can I be a part of this world? I was 28.

Berlin (West), Berlin (East)

West Berlin in those years was edgy, raw, and decadent, because obscenely pampered: arts and industry funded by Western money, the male students there not amenable to the otherwise universal West German draft, the looming presence of the Wall inspiring to a kind of seductive, if ultimately shallow, nihilism, both cultural and political. We were pawns in Berlin, and we knew it: this gave us the freedom to thumb our nose at the world, both at our protectors the West and our strange refracted image the East, no less in thrall to its own Big Power than we were to ours.

We were enclosed by the East, and were conscious of it in the very air we breathed. The infinitely poorer and environmentally incorrect East (just how much poorer and how environmentally incorrect we had to wait till its dissolution to see, to everyone's collective horror) heated its houses with "brown coal," bituminous coal which I inhaled while doing my jogging around one of the two artificial mountains made from piled up WW II rubble in the confines of West Berlin and covered with a so-thin layer of dirt and grass. When the wind blew in our direction we became part of this sulfurous world, cut only by the smells of the Western brewery or the chocolate factory. Their cars, laughable tin cans (or rather, in the case of the ubiquitous Trabant, plastic ones) puffed noxious half-burned vapors that wafted over the Wall into the West when the wind was right—or wrong. Now Trabis have become collectors items, part of a general "Ostalgie." Nostalgia is inevitable: we treasure the past merely because it was, it's more solid than the future, and it can't be changed. Sartre was right: we all aspire to the status of the past, and never attain it.

The East looked different too, the first thing people noticed when they went over: with its faded, gray streets; faded, gray people all dressed in drab; buildings with bullet-pocked façades; courtyards that seemed unchanged from the years of Weimar. The all but empty store windows, such as the "Lederwaren [Leather Goods]" store Unter den Linden with a few unfashionable handbags of plastic fading in the wan sunlight and the pyramids of canned Cuban pineapple in the "Delicatessen" stores wrapped in pale yellow paper, all of it guarded with checkpoints and police, with back-ups at the border for trunk searches, sub-machine-gun-toting soldiers and the perennial demand for documents.

I went into the East as a West Berliner, with my residence permit, though like all non-East Germans I had to change 25 DM at the not-so-arbitrary face-saving East-set exchange rate of one to one. In Western banks you could get ten times that, but you weren't allowed to bring it in. The day-trip visa was good until midnight. Many evenings I would gather my things in the Brecht Theater (Berliner Ensemble) by the Spree after yet another Weimar-acidic performance of works by that disaffected master Brecht (best theater in either of the Berlins, I thought) that had run very late, walk through the quiet side streets to the rotting, moldy Friedrichstraße train station, hurrying if midnight was nigh, run the gauntlet of the green-garbed guards sitting behind counters in their fluorescent booths rigged with mirrors to check that I was not hiding someone at my feet, descending the ugly green corridors of the train station to the track for the West Berlin subway that made its sole stop in a loop from the other side of the Wall, under East Berlin, and back into the West, and be dazzled anew as it pulled up, a blazing world of colored advertisements, yellow lights, and brightly dressed people that I entered to be whisked away from the drab world of the East back into the full-colored reality of the West On the way back into the West, the train would slow without stopping at all the other stations under the East on that line, to reveal in half-gloom gun-toting soldiers at these now-barricaded points of contact, their walls still decorated with posters from August, 1961 fresh and still eternally new in the continual near-darkness.

West Berliners could get day-trip visas into East Germany as well. I went to Dresden to see the Zwinger, the famous Semper Opera, and Semper's yet more famous Picture Gallery and its contents. Here was the hollow dampness of the train station, of side streets with ruins still left over from the bombardment, of the Prager Straße that led to the pile of rubble that had once been the Marienkirche, lined with ugly aluminum-colored Stalinist boxes and the odd faux-classy café where one could sip bitter near-coffee that came from a different world than the steaming cups of strong brew of the West, in which the thick cream, served in a little silver pitcher, made swirls, and the tiny bar of velvety chocolate that could be immersed in the coffee until it too dissolved into aromatic shreds.

Further afield, I discovered Prague, a city whose beauty can compare only with Paris or Petersburg (I think of them now as the P-cities), but which then seemed doomed to carry out its sentence of slow dissolution, the beautiful Art Nouveau façades of all the houses on the "Mala Strana" slowly cracking and peeling with time, poor maintenance, and the general Communist cold. I went to Moscow and Leningrad, as it still was then, indistinguishable from the German tourists around me but feeling that as an American I was truly tasting the unknown.

The East back then seemed another world. Its existence as such seemed ineluctable, something that merely had to be accepted, and could not be changed. No one I knew in Berlin would, they have since told me, have ever been able to predict the fall of the Wall. For us the division of Europe into two was a given, a fact we accepted, like saying that we human beings have two arms. We took it for granted and went on; it defined our lives but for that reason left us free to do other things.

I have since walked through the Brandenburg Gate from the West Berlin Tiergarten, onto the still dumpy Unter den Linden, once the 5th Avenue of Berlin but in the post-War years a moldy dead end swarming with Eastern policemen, the dreaded Vopos (Volkspolizisten), bounded by the No Man's Land between the two layers of Wall, at the time reportedly mined. When the Wall fell we discovered it wasn't. For someone who never knew it otherwise, this walk through the Gate must seem the most natural thing in the world.

Anything can change, all is flux. Now, only the fact that the East has become banal in the throes of its post-Communist re-birth (or whatever it is that is happening there) may somehow mitigate the fact that it was precisely my position as a pampered outsider in no real danger of ever being held captive on the wrong side that made it all so fascinating.

Givens

By the time I left Berlin I knew what an East European capital was going to look like, even if I hadn't seen it yet: the smells, the gray building fronts, the Soviet block apartments on the way from the train station, the feel of the paper, the pre-Soviet buildings in the Altstadt. I had been in enough of them that I knew beforehand the grainy taste of the chocolate, the lack of fresh fruit, the bitterness of the coffee. What had at first been fascinating, an alternative universe, acquired its own banality. Once again, I'd used up the exotic.

Still, there was no way I could simply melt into this world—nor would I want to. It was too deprived, too gray. They knew by looking at me that I didn't belong: I was a rich "Wessie," a Western foreigner. I could look, but they looked back. I was always glad to go back to West Berlin where I could once again melt into the crowd. Finally, in Rwanda, I found a world so alien from one I was comfortable in I could not even think of "passing." It was at this point that I was ready to come back home, and shoulder the responsibility of marriage and step-children. Indeed, by the time I left Rwanda at age 33 I was hungry for responsibility, having been weightless for too long, a giant balloon tethered to the ground only by the slimmest of threads, in danger of floating off at the slightest breeze. Why be here? Why, for that matter, be there? I longed for roots to tether me to the Earth, a reason for being in one place rather than another.

In having been able to travel and live in different places before I decided on my own to stay put, I have been given a great gift: I was able to learn what Emerson tried to tell stay-at-homes. You take yourself with you everywhere you go. At the same time, you discover who you are. You figure out what can change and what can't. I have displaced myself to the point where I know what the hierarchy of my givens is. Once travel was part of my education; now it's only a pastime. Most people are so anchored to the givens of their situation—as I was not, but later became—bound by marriage, say, or children, or jobs, or commitments to specific places, they can never allow themselves to let out the line enough to find out what could be changed. If asked, they would say they are who they are. And so they are. If they altered some things in their situations, of course, they might find out they were different than what they thought they were. About ourselves, we learn the things we are allowed by our circumstances to learn. If the circumstances change, we learn other things.

I learned by seeing Martha react to an unstable demanding child during our marriage that she held adult relationships in general, and our marriage in particular, for naught. She would have sacrificed our whole world—and in fact, did so—to the whims, not even the needs, of a problematic child later diagnosed as never having separated her personality from that of her mother. Without the child, would I ever have learned this about Martha? Could we still be married, my respect and love for her undimmed? Can I imagine Martha without her problematic daughter? Who we are, and what we know about ourselves, are the result of chance. All of us have paths not taken in our lives. Way leads on to way, as Frost puts it in "The Road Not Taken." You don't get to go back and walk the paths you didn't.

Why I'm Not in the Foreign Service

Much later I was reminded of one such path I might, it seemed, have taken, but didn't. Thinking about this step made me nostalgic for my younger, pre-Martha self: nostalgic, and at the same time acutely aware that that person was now dead, having been killed by the realization that all is not in fact possible for the motivated individual, and that some problems will by their very nature end up defeating us. A sudden resolve to clean out the metallic gray hulk of the filing cabinet in a corner of my bedroom produced, in addition to a disordered heap of decade-old phone bills and the equally disordered records of a small and now non-existent account with a small and now non-existent bank, a cache of correspondence from 1987, with the Board of Examiners of the Foreign Service. Before throwing it all away, I re-read these testaments to a vanished desire, an ill-advised attempt to spend my life drifting from post to post in a series of third-world capitals, Port au Prince or Mogadishu, rather than sitting comfortably in Annapolis.

The reason I didn't join the Foreign Service was sex: an affair I had had some years earlier with a Hungarian woman named Eva.

I met Eva in 1982, shortly before I went to Siena and then to Berlin, on the north porch of Chartres Cathedral. As I came out of the darkened nave of the church into the bright sunlight, leaning against the heavy door, I heard a group of women singing a folk-song type chanson in a language I couldn't identify. Blinking against the sudden light, I suddenly became conscious of one who seemed the leader of the group, large-hipped and attractive, her head covered in the tight curls and wearing big sunglasses. They sang; I wandered off. Suddenly the woman with the sunglasses was at my elbow.

"These look older than the others," she said, gesturing at the row of saints and Biblical figures on the columns.

"Actually they're the newest ones on the cathedral," I said. "And how did you know I spoke English?"

"Oh," she said roguishly, continuing in her perfect British English with a touch of Cockney, "you're such a tall bloke I figured you were English. Or American. You're American, aren't you?"

"Yes," I said, amused. "How about you?"

"Hungarian," she said.

"Where did you learn English?" I asked, conversationally I hoped, to indicate that I met Hungarians every day.

Years before I'd driven through Hungary and seen Budapest, with my longtime Parisian friend, the one whose apartment I later borrowed so often. It all seemed terribly exotic. We'd gone on a trip from Paris in a 2CV, south to Italy, via ferry to Greece, north into the oncoming fall into what was then Yugoslavia and Hungary, then back into the West through Austria and Germany and back to Paris. Before crossing the border from Greece I burned all my notes and hid personal papers, my friend having said that they might search us. On the Fischerbastei in Budapest scruffy young men would pass us head-down, murmuring gutterally "Change dollars? Jeans for sale?" When we crossed the border into Austria, I breathed a sigh of relief.

"My father worked at the Hungarian Embassy in London when I was a child," the woman said.

"Oh," I said.

"I've got to go," she said. "We're going back to Paris."

"So am I," I said.

"Well then," she said brightly, "let me give you my address. Call me at this number, it's a student hostel."

I liked her directness, and I thought it was fun to be picked up by a Hungarian woman on the steps of Chartres Cathedral. Go with opportunities, you never know where they'll lead—that was my motto. Besides, it made my dick hard to have a pretty girl display such evident interest in me. Yes: we speak the same language, and I don't mean English.

I did call that night from Paris, and after an interminable wait with much incomprehensible back and forth on the other end, got her on the line, whereupon we made a date to meet on the steps of the Opéra the next day at noon sharp.

The next day I was there at 5 of 12. 12 o'clock came and went, then 12:15, then almost 12:30. I began to think she was going to stand me up. This puzzled me, given her evident interest in making the date. Perhaps she had been held up. Or had she had second thoughts? Could it all have been a cruel trick? Surely I had not been so off base in reading the signals?

Just when I had just given up thinking she would come, she was there, hurrying up the steps. Breathless, she gave me a story of missed busses and smiled at me. My dick reared its head in my pants; I smiled back.

We walked in the Tuileries, sat at a table and drank *citron pressé*. She was in Paris studying French, she told me. She taught English at the Karl-Marx-Institute for Economics in Budapest. She was here on a scholarship from her government. In the West everything was "horribly dear." We looked at the people strolling by under the *marroniers*. I asked if she'd like to go to the Comédie Française that night. She said yes, and we walked across the street from the park to the theater. I bought tickets. For an instant I resented her not offering to pay her share. Yet she had made it perfectly clear that she was living on a shoestring; everything was expensive in the West and she could afford nothing that was not already part of her scholarship. Besides, it was all too clear that this was a quid pro quo; the man paid for the evening's pre-entertainment. We parted, I to go back to my friend's place and she to return to her hostel to change.

That night we amused ourselves in the back row of the Comédie Française by seeing how many places on each other we could put our hands and still remain within the bounds of decency. The play, I recall, amusingly enough for me, was Molière's *Don Juan*, one of his lesser efforts. Or perhaps I just wasn't paying attention.

Eva spent the night with me, and the next. The sex was stellar. "My ex-husband told me I was frigid," she said.

"Not with me," I replied smugly.

"Not with you," she agreed.

The last morning I was leaving to go to Siena for the summer, prior to going up to Berlin. I had to get up early, and so did she. I wanted to give her a goodbye present. I knew that what she wanted most was money to pay for a visa she had talked of having to pay in francs. But how to avoid the appearance of paying for sex and so turning her into a prostitute? We were fairly close to that line as it was. I folded the bill up to an unrecognizable scrap and dropped it on her breakfast plate. "One visa coming up," I said. "Sunny-side-up." I wondered if her English extended to knowing what "sunny-side-up" meant. In any case, she clapped her hands delightedly and kissed me, then dropped the unfolded scrap into her pocketbook.

I gave her a kiss before we each got into our taxi in front of the apartment where I was staying. "Write to me," she said. "Maybe you can visit from Berlin."

"Yes," I said. "I'd like that."

I had a wonderful summer in Siena. Then the summer was over, and on the other side of the Alps, the leaves had begun to change.

Once in Berlin, I phoned Eva. She seemed delighted to hear from me. Knowing she was in Budapest made her even more exotic. I wondered fleetingly how much I was playing for her the role of the exotic foreigner from the Golden West.

Where could we meet? That was a problem. Hungarians were allowed visas only to even more repressive Czechoslovakia. Even East Germany, with its proximity to West Berlin, was forbidden. We agreed, therefore, to meet in Prague, though both of us were clear it would have to be after Christmas. That was fine. I had become involved with other women, though I had memories of great sex in Paris and wanted to keep her on the list. But Prague, it turned out, was expensive, and I too was living on a fellowship. If I simply came to Budapest, we could, she said when I called her back to report, stay in her apartment. We set up a week in March when we were both free. I hung up the phone and smiled.

Christmas came and went. I bought a ticket on the East German airline Interflug that left from East Berlin to Budapest. Two weeks later I left West Berlin for the East on the surprisingly modern Hungarian-made Icarus bus that picked up passengers for Schönefeld, only a few hundred meters over the Wall south of the city in East Germany. Even for this brief transit on East German soil we needed a visa, whose point was to collect the 5 DM that were demanded as a fee. The Vopos entered the bus with clipboards to collect our Western passports and the moon-like discs of 5 DM pieces, and the one stamped and the other collected, we were ferried across the railroad tracks to the dingy terminal of the airport, full of short Eastern European people with bad teeth carrying plastic luggage cracking at the seams.

The wings on the Russian-made propeller airplane that took me to Budapest droned so loudly I could hardly hear myself think. The inside of the cabin had been painted so often the walls were peeling; a storage bin in the bathroom wouldn't close properly and paper towels spilled from the wire trash can. The Eastern chocolate served with the meal was gritty. It was different; I liked it for that reason.

It was sunny and spring-like in Budapest, in contrast to cold and gray Berlin I'd left back in the North. Eva met me at the airport, immediately hugging me as if she'd only said good-by the day before, talking volubly, steering me to the subway. We emerged somewhere near downtown; from there we took a bus. I allowed myself to be led; in any case had no choice but to follow. The bus drove along the Danube, Eva pointed out the neo-Gothic City Hall whose cousins I had seen in Vienna and Munich, the churches, the domes, the outline of Buda Castle behind us.

Suddenly she touched my arm. "We get off here," she said. We got off, the other passengers smiling at us and our English.

We walked through endless slabs of modern apartment buildings till suddenly she touched my arm again. "Here," she said. "Through here."

We cut around the end of another building, she guided me up the steps, we turned left once inside the door, and were suddenly inside her tiny apartment with pull-out day bed, miniature bathtub, and canister-like water heater. I dropped my bags, she pulled off my coat, our mouths turned inside out, and within seconds she was on the floor, with my dick, whose erection had been on hold all day in the airplane waiting for this moment, inside of her.

We made love several times a day on the floor and in her narrow bed. We walked by the Danube and bumped hips as we walked. We went to museums and put our hands inside each others' clothes while we looked at the paintings.

We even, to give it all the stamp of respectability, visited her parents in their larger apartment in a new part of town, great slabs of apartment blocks set in sand by the side of the Danube, apartments made with brighter window fittings and furnished with newer furnishings. I got along well with her father, who didn't seem to mind at all that I was sleeping with his daughter, and was a cultivated man who told me what Hungarian poets to read, talked to me about the American "cosmonauts" who had done this and so, and who showed the civilized man's appreciation of what topics to avoid because likely to produce disagreement. I pegged him as a loyal Party man, if one who had seen too much of the world to really be convinced, and a fierce patriot. I met Eva's brother, rosy-cheeked in his Hungarian army uniform; we shook hands warily and he, speaking no English, went off to his barracks, leaving us to have dinner with Mom and Dad in the cheery kitchen of their flat. Clearly he was less than thrilled to be meeting Eva's American boyfriend—or whatever I was.

In the evenings we went, Eva and I, to plays: to a lovely children's musical that Eva whispered the plot of in my ear, something with singing and dancing houseplants; to *A Streetcar Named Desire*, of course in Hungarian; to the worst performance of Balanchine I have ever seen, a version of *Agon* with all the edges rounded so utterly it looked like putty and where the theater emptied out so quickly after the performance I was left alone in the lobby, the last person to collect his hat and coat from the dumpy hat-check woman stationed in her window by the door, feeling that somehow I had finally come to the faded heart of Mitteleuropa.

For someone with access to DM or dollars, Budapest was inexpensive. Even I, on a Fulbright, could afford the best restaurants here, if not back home in Berlin. And it was in the restaurants that I realized that Eva was speaking English not merely for my benefit, but for that of the people around her. In fact, it suddenly became clear to me, after about the second time out, that she didn't want the waiters even to realize that she was Hungarian; here she was English. Though never leaving her home city, Eva too was playing tourist, trying out the role of the visiting Englishwoman with her good-looking equally foreign boyfriend, visitors from the Other world, the West that Hungarians still so clearly longed to re-join, lopped off by fiat at the end of a now long-ago war. Of course, this was merely tit for tat, as I was playing a role too. For me, it was the American in the East. It was easy for me to play it, as I had gotten to leave home; here she was stuck among all the things she already knew.

Though we had sex constantly, if not nearly often enough for me, I was not even sure at the time that Eva found me particularly attractive. We stopped one day, walking along, outside a nightclub, decorated at the entrance with come-on photos of the girls.

"Do you like them?" she asked me, smiling roguishly.

"Of course," I said. They were, like nightclub girls the world over, attractive, at least in pictures.

"They have more boobs than I do," she observed generously, using "boobs" in a collective plural to mean, chest size rather than separable units, say three breasts rather than two.

"Yes," I said. I wouldn't have brought it up, but it was true. Eva had wide hips, which was good in my book. But she was also endowed with small, almost pear-like breasts, oddly out of proportion with her otherwise generous measurements.

"They're more the Hungarian female beauty ideal than I am," she observed dispassionately.

I decided to live dangerously. "And what's the Hungarian male beauty ideal?" I asked. "At all like me?"

She apprised me reflectively, then smiled. "You're a bit on the thin side," she said finally—as if to say, let's leave it at that. And then she linked her arm in mine.

It was the beginning of spring. The weeping willows along the Danube were flecked with wispy green buds. I noted all the couples walking along like us, and held Eva as tight as she was holding me. One day we went north, to Visegrad, the remains of a Medieval fort. I remember the strengthening sun, though still not hot enough to allow to take off my jacket. Back in town, we went shopping in the chic street, the Vaci Utca, where I bought a dozen Hungaratron Bartók records and some embroidery, which, back in the West, I gave away as gifts.

And then our time was up. Though Eva had been smiling and compliant the entire week, she did not seem cast down at my going. I made her a final present of a nearly-full bottle of hand cream; I had brought her other Western things as presents when I came. "I'd hoped you'd leave that," she said, and gave me a smile.

She had insisted on accompanying me to the airport, and on getting dressed up to do it. The computer at the Malev desk, which also handled the Interflug flights, was down, so my ticket was processed by hand. We kissed and hugged. I promised to call. I crossed the barrier separating passengers from accompanyers, and turned around to wave goodbye. And here I made a mistake. Perhaps this mistake wasn't the first in our week together, but it was the one that confirmed so much I had suspected about us. Thinking her looking somewhat forlorn on her side of the barrier whereas I was getting on a plane to return to my pocket of affluence in the West—though she was smartly decked out in a scarf and spring blouse under which I could see her breasts—I reached back as if to touch her fingers one last time in what must have been intended as a gesture of tenderness, or perhaps pity. Or was it something as simple as guilt?

At my motion, her smile flickered. I realized she was puzzled: what was I up to now? When her arm moved in response, it was in a sudden jerk, as if from a dead stop, her body curving, but out of line, somehow not in the direction I had assumed it would. Then she seemed to figure out what I had in mind, and her arm rose to meet my gesture, the smile now securely on her face; we touched palms and fingers one last time and I turned and moved on.

For me this gesture may have been a belated post scriptum, an expression of something I could not otherwise express, an acknowledgement that people use people and that's just the way it is, and that I acknowledged the unfairness of the world that had dealt us so unequal a hand. For me as for her a fling, yes. The difference was, I got to go back to the West.

For Eva, the last adieu had already been exchanged, and I was already on the plane back to my world, leaving her in hers. Her vacation at any rate would last until she got off the bus in front of her apartment house and went in and changed clothes again. Or would she keep the smart scarf on all afternoon, and speak English to the bus driver on the way back into town?

A few hours later, having navigated flight, airport, and the crossing of the Wall, I was back home. The next day, I called her to thank her for a lovely time. We chatted, she seemed happy, I promised to write. I did so, idle gossip that would pass whatever censor decided to be interested, and tried to call several times in the ensuing weeks. The phone rang and rang. Finally, one day a month or so later, it picked up, and a strange male voice answered, responding angrily and incomprehensibly in Hungarian to my demands in English, German, French, and Italian, to speak with Eva. The phone was slammed down, and I was left with a buzzing in my ear.

A month or so later Eva wrote to say that she was engaged to a former student, much younger than she. Her parents disapproved. The fiancé was jealous; perhaps it would be better if I didn't call. A year later she sent me a Christmas card saying her father had died; I sent a letter of condolence to her mother, and one to her. And that was the last I heard.

Annapolis

From Berlin, I went to Freiburg, spending most of my weekends in Italy, Switzerland, Austria, and Alsace. No problem, to be French, or Italian, or even German, to live my life in those languages, to take for granted another world of food, of authors, of expressions for my sentiments. By now I could do all that. But in Rwanda, where I went after Freiburg, I realized I came from another world. I have come full circle in my life, back to Maryland, only to find myself among an alien, if likeable, race of people. Here at Annapolis, people believe that individuals are the masters of their own destiny; "motivation" conquers all. I know this not to be true. The world I live in today is as strange to me as anything I saw in Africa.

Arrived here in Annapolis, now home for twenty years, there was the old business of the Foreign Service Exam, something I had signed up for in far-off Kigali, even before I'd gotten the job at Annapolis that brought me back to Maryland. By this time the possibility of living in a series of sad third-world countries as a hard-working bird in a gilded cage, not to mention the mouthpiece of U.S. policy I disagreed with and in any case was not responsible for, seemed distinctly less than alluring. I was in love with Martha by this point, tired of moving about, ready to have a family. In insisting on following up this test I was, I think, merely carrying out the desires of a person I had ceased to be, or tying up a loose thread in my life.

The test for the Foreign Service consists, or at least consisted at the time, of several parts. The written part is followed by an oral one, which can only be taken in Washington. Applicants are tested in groups of about 10. The kind of people who think the Foreign Service would be a good idea are a type, clean-faced preppy sorts, male and female, graduates of "good colleges." When I saw my fellow testees that morning, boys and girls right out of school, I felt old, being a Ph.D. already into my 30s.

The first part of the test is a simulation affair: the group is given a problem and time to discuss it. We were to hold a staff meeting at the American Embassy in Erehwon (somebody had fun writing this part of the test, taking the name of the country from Samuel Butler's utopian novel title, Nowhere-spelled-backwards) and must decide whether to fund a pipeline or the library. Another part of the ordeal was the legendary, and universally dreaded, "in-basket" test, an exercise in virtuality, half fictional, half very real. It consisted of a manila envelope with the contents of what I finally understood to be the "in" basket, pronounced with the emphasis on the proposition (as opposed to, "out-basket"; initially I thought it was the opposite of "in-somewhere-else," e.g. in the trash can) of a fictional diplomat in country X.

This diplomat having been called away, each of us, on opening his or her envelope, was the substitute called in to deal with the accumulated correspondence of our absent colleague. The helicopter would arrive for us in an hour and a half, not coincidentally exactly the time we had to finish the test, to take us back to the capital, by which time we had to have sorted things into Essential, Somewhat Essential, Less Essential, Trivial, and Forget It—and have dealt, in some fashion, with as much of the pile as we could deal with.

In the version of the in-basket test I took, there was a group of nuns much incensed because the man they had been employing as their gardener had been run over by an Embassy driver. The test-makers had been having fun here as well, as a "Tracy Lord" (the Katherine Hepburn role in *The Philadelphia Story*) figured prominently. In the envelope, the very real simulation of this fictional in-basket, were faux-handwritten scrawls, faux-letterheads, and faux-memos, all to be dealt with in a very real time limit, delineated by the fictional clock in country X as inexorably as the real clock in this office building in Washington.

It was like unraveling a mystery. You were supposed to figure out by the bottom of the stack that the man the nuns were so upset about was the same man whom the Minister of Foreign Affairs had inquired about, or some such; all the threads linked, and you were supposed (I imagine) to deal with it through "proper channels," and (say) put off consoling the nuns until you had answered the Minister. Or perhaps God's call was more important than Caesar's; who knows. I'm not sure I know even now what the right answer was. All I know is, I passed. Yet the subsequent medical tests showed that I was still affected by the Hepatitis A I had brought out of Africa as its parting gift (it turns your eyes yellow and your shits white), and that I would have to be re-checked in some months.

And then there was the security clearance. The problem was Eva. The problem for the Foreign Service with my involvement with her, apparently, was not so much my having had the affair, but acknowledging it when asked, or perhaps, not acknowledging enough, or with the proper tone of voice. This acknowledgment on my part, in response to a direct question on a written form, Had I ever had sexual relations with citizens of East Bloc countries?, led to several endless interviews with poker-faced FBI agents clearly used to getting their own way, whose conclusion was that I was "surly and uncooperative" (a written assessment I saw years later as a result of a Freedom of Information Act request) when I assured them that the affair was by then long ago, that the woman had remarried and asked me not to call her again, and that I had no intention of giving them her address so they could go bother her and her new husband. I added that furthermore I thought I had shown extreme cooperation in answering truthfully. Since, I pointed out, I clearly had nothing to hide, and because more fundamentally I had not lied to them about having had the affair, surely they would take my word for it that the affair was private, over, and no possible threat to anyone.

Apparently this reasoning was specious. Though by then I had cleared all of the not inconsiderable hurdles, I was denied a security clearance as a bad risk. As a result, my candidacy for the Foreign Service was "terminated": I liked the suggestion of sudden, silent death that the word evoked. And I found out why only when I demanded my application materials much later. My anger at reading the verdict in black and white on sheets of paper punch-stamped UNCLASSIFIED was leavened by bemusement at the repeated black-outs with felt-tipped pen of parts of the interviews with the FBI agents. As a bad security risk, it was evident I couldn't be trusted with seeing the whole contents of my own interviews. No wonder novels like *Catch-22* have such a long shelf life.

I decided I didn't in any case want to be part of an organization that thought this way. And eventually, after the initial shock, I settled into Annapolis, having perhaps finally found what I had been looking for all along: a foreign country whose very strangeness could delight me in a thousand small ways every day, and yet where no one knew I was a foreigner, so that I would be merely left alone to enjoy things and not be beset by beggars and small boys. Still, several years later, after the fall of the Berlin Wall, when Hungarian citizenship no longer carried the negative charge for the FBI it once had, I contacted the Foreign Service about having this black mark removed from the consideration process. I was told that I was welcome to apply like the thousands of other hopefuls and take my chances in a new round of applications. But the old application, having been "terminated," could not be revived. It was then that I decided definitively that my life path had after all, been taken, that I would cease looking back at what might have been, and tell myself that I really was, rather than merely going through the motions as an Assistant Professor of English at the U.S. Naval Academy. The fates, or at least the Board of Examiners of the Foreign Service (not to mention the Federal Bureau of Investigation) had spoken: so should it thenceforth be. Another thing to add to my shadow CV of jobs I did not get, places I did not go.

Four
A Thousand Hills

I came back to the States from Berlin not quite knowing what was to become of me. One day that muggy Washington summer I had gone jogging on the Washington Mall from Keith's house. When I got back, I found a phone message. A professor in Germany had called to offer me a job. My dissertation advisor had sent in my name for a sort of low-level faculty exchange program that Vanderbilt had traditionally staffed. I hadn't even known I was being proposed. Having nothing else, I accepted.

Freiburg turned out to be agreeably international, though tucked into the Black Forest. In 45 minutes I could be in either Strasbourg or Basel. In two hours I could be in Zurich, in four in Milan. Anything was possible with a car, an old red Russian-made Fiat called a Lada I drove as far down as Florence in one direction, and Cordoba in another. I took three-day weekends and was never at home. This idyll of exploration lasted two years.

In Freiburg, I applied for a Fulbright post in Beijing. I was rejected almost immediately. (Add that to my shadow-CV.) When I asked why, I was told that China was a very popular destination, and that furthermore the fact that I was already living "outside the country" (outside the U.S., that is; I could have pointed out I was certainly living inside *some* country) had counted against me. The Fulbright people, it seemed, were looking for corn-fed professors who had never left Iowa to spread the unadulterated gospel of American culture. Still, the Fulbright people said, they had noticed I spoke French; perhaps they could forgive my international taint. Would I possibly be interested in Rwanda? I nearly threw the letter in the trash can. The world that I knew did not include sub-Saharan Africa, which largely lacked opera houses, museums, and, I thought, livable cities. Thinking it might be fun after all, the next week I re-wrote my protestations of how much I wanted to go to China, changing them into equally fervent professions of interest in Central Africa.

Rwanda is a country the size of Maryland, or Albania, lying east of the Congo and east of Lake Victoria. Rwanda calls itself, with justice, "The Country of a Thousand Hills." It's composed of ridge after ridge of sloping, finger-like folds covered with patch-work farm plots and dotted with banana trees. With neighboring Congo, then Zaire, it shares the highest lake in Africa, Kivu, one of the chain of great lakes that extends along the Rift Valley from Uganda to Malawi. In the northeast of Rwanda begins the chain of volcanoes which are home to the gorillas; yet further to the north, between Uganda and the Congo, lie the Rwenzori, or "Mountains of the Moon," where the Egyptians thought the source of the Nile was to be found. That's where I lived. The university campus where taught was, it turned out, hours away from the city, in the middle of potato fields spread out spectacularly at the foot of a range of volcanoes that ranged between Rwanda, The Congo, and Uganda.

It can only be the lakes of Rwanda, and perhaps its mountains, that prompted the national tourist office, at least before the killings of 1994, to advertise the country as "the Switzerland of Africa." Aside from its landscape, size, and its landlocked situation, Rwanda is the very antithesis of Switzerland: pre-industrial, isolated, and its population predominantly illiterate. Life in the hills goes on largely as it did hundreds of years ago.

Since the slaughter of 1994 is what people nowadays know about Rwanda—killings that occurred when I was going through the hell of my divorce from Martha back in quaint Annapolis, so that my experience of a beautiful sleepy corner of the world seemed in retrospect like the calm before the storm, like taking refuge on an island that turns out to be set on the back of a sleeping sea monster—it's useful to point out that a good deal of history preceded them.

For centuries Rwanda was ruled by the tall people from the North, the Tutsi, who, though never more than about 10% of the population, lorded it over the indigenous Hutu. In 1959, just before independence, the majority Hutu overthrew their overlords. Many of the Tutsi fled to Uganda; some stayed on as cattle farmers. Now the Tutsi have returned to power after having been held from it for more than three decades. It was the military victories of the advancing Tutsi who, in 1990, invaded the country from their base in Uganda with the complicity of the expansionist Uganda president Museveni (the West's golden boy, and hence beyond criticism), that led to the slaughter in 1994 by radical Hutu not eager to be ruled again by Tutsi. The minority Tutsis, who ruled Rwanda's twin country to the south, Burundi, had staged periodic purges of their local Hutus several times during the post-independence years.

The impetus for the 1994 slaughter in Rwanda was the downing of an airplane with the Rwandan president and those of several other surrounding countries, returning from peace talks in Tanzania at which he had been forced to cede some power to the invading Tutsis, who had been repeatedly winning on the battlefield. Speculation is still that it was hard-line Hutus opposed to ceding this power to the invaders who unleashed the "genocide"—in quotation marks because moderate Hutus were targeted along with the Tutsis who had never left Rwanda for either Uganda or Zaire. Grisly though they were, the killings were political, not those of a "people" ("genocide"). And now the Tutsi regime, finally victorious on the battlefield, has expanded into the Congo, felling the "kleptocracy" of the long-time dictator Mobutu, and then turning on the dictator who, with Tutsi/Rwandan support, overthrew him. Just because the murderers of the 1994 rampages were Hutus doesn't mean the Tutsis were "good guys," despite what the Anglophone press has chosen to believe.

Indeed, it was Western, specifically American, press coverage of Rwanda that convinced me conservatives are right who criticize the "bias" of the media. In this case, it was clear that everything was seen through American glasses. Say "minority" to a well-meaning American journalist, and they hear "powerless, victim." It somehow passed notice that the particular minority in question had held almost feudal sway over Rwandans for centuries. Anything that was a minority was good, and deserved defense. That's the way we do things in the West, after all; that this might be different doesn't seem to have crossed anyone's mind.

Some revisionist historians have claimed it was the Belgians who had "created" the difference between Hutus and Tutsis, making a distinction of jobs (the Tutsi, like other tall people in Kenya, were cattle farmers; Tutsi poetry deals with the beauty of cows) into one of "race" that appeared on their national identity cards. Some have even questioned whether the Tutsi came from Somalia, as they are held to have done—the details of migration are lost in the mists of what for that part of the world is pre-history, and seem largely based on visual speculation.

But the revisionists can't show the standard story isn't true, and what remains is the fact that within living memory the Tutsi were oppressive overlords, and had been so for centuries. If the distinction between Tutsi and Hutu was in fact a colonial fabrication, it was one that "took" in the Rwandan mind. For them, it *was* a racial distinction, with a few obvious exceptions (occasional short Tutsis). The postulate that there had been a pre-colonial time when both sides lived in harmony is as much a dream as the Garden of Eden.

Brigadoon

Rwanda between 1962 and 1990 had slumbered peacefully among its hills, a Brigadoon that was not yet ready to reawake to its date with violence. The university had asked for an American professor, and the government had seconded the request. I went there to work, not as a tourist. The world around me was therefore real. My job was to come to terms with this reality.

Though the university was run by and for Rwandans, it too was a Western institution, and a recently-imported one at that, set up by the Belgians after independence and largely paid for by the Canadians. The language in which I was asked to teach, English, was foreign as well. The local Bantu language is the fiendishly difficult Kinyarwanda, and my students had added French (then the country's official colonial language) only in high school. Before coming to the university they had some instruction in English. After graduation from the "second cycle," five years in all, most of them would return to these schools to teach

English themselves. Some few might, with luck, become bureaucrats in the capital, Kigali, or enter the diplomatic service if they had the proper connections.

This campus of the university was an unprepossessing collection of one-story brick buildings joined together by concrete sidewalks, rather like a low-key American high school. They were plopped down in the middle of the potato fields—situated in so isolated a spot because it was the home area of the president, the one whose plane went down in 1994, eight kilometers from the closest town. (It wasn't too oppressive, but it was essentially a one-party state.) The town, Ruhengeri, was and I suppose is a one-story line-up of shops like a wild-West town, in the foothills of the volcanoes that I saw from my back yard. Here I sat, reading Shakespeare and Jane Austen. It wasn't the "heart of darkness." It was just Anywhere. I was contented. After all, Europe had become a bit passé for me, because I could "pass" too well: countries and cultures that had once set my blood hopping now seemed to me merely other flavors of normalcy. What was the point of going to (say) Provence if all it meant was that you had to find something to do, now that the fabric of life itself wasn't exotic?

In Rwanda *I* was what was exotic. When I jogged along the rutted, unpaved roads of dust and volcanic stones, the little boys herding cattle cried out "mzungu! mzungu!" as I passed (white man! white man!). The old women, their hair issuing from the forehead bands betokening their status as married women, merely stood and stared. My skin color telegraphed my foreignness, my much greater wealth, my freedom to leave by getting on the Air France and soaring away, like a marooned spaceman who finally succeeds in fixing his lamed ship and disappearing.

In such a world, even I was unable to live without falling into the trap of what Orwell calls "la danse du pukka sahib," the necessity for the colonialist to play a role rather than merely carry on with life. Everything I did was an attempt to prove a point, to live "normally" for my world, not for theirs. It was as if I were a man-to-woman transsexual living every moment "as a woman"—something a person born female would never have to do. She could merely live. The tiger does not express its *tigritude,* as Wole Soyinka noted as a response to Leopold Senghor's notion of *négritude*; it merely does what it does. Precisely this was what was impossible for me in Rwanda. I was condemned to expressing my *blanchitude.*

Of course, all of us in semi-public positions such as a professor must keep up appearances and do nothing to dishonor the uniform, as the Navy puts it. Yet there is a time when we take off the uniform and can relax. In Rwanda there was no respite, no place where the mask could come off. For even with other "Europeans," as (white) Westerners are called in Africa, we were conscious of living an artificial life 24/7. The mayonnaise I brought back from Paris and ate for lunch with friends seemed a major victory over my surroundings—and was commented on as such (it was difficult to get home-made mayonnaise to "gel" at our mile-high altitude, despite my cook's best efforts). The classical music I played on tapes on the portable speakers that stowed so neatly into my carry-on was a sign that the rest of the world existed and could be exported even here. (Civilization is anything you can take with you on the Air France.) Every time I got into my bathtub whose water came from an Italian water heater, I reflected on how pampered I was.

It was life lived out in capital letters, majuscules. In the morning I sat in the banana-leaf gazebo my ingenious house "boy" Florien (a twenty-something married man with two children) had constructed one vacation using my Swiss Army knife and his own ingenuity, listening to the BBC World Service, eating toast and papaya. (Foreigners shared important information, like where to buy things like bread for toast—the Church-run store in Ruhengeri, and cheese—a Belgian operation on the road to Gisenyi, and edible non-tough chickens—a project about 30 miles away.) I wasn't merely eating breakfast in my gazebo, I was Eating Breakfast In My Gazebo, here in Central Africa. When I drove my Suzuki 4 x 4 down the rutted roads or on the surprisingly good Chinese-constructed highway to Kigali, I wasn't merely getting from point A to point B, I was Driving a Car in Rwanda: at least the gaping stares of the barefoot peasants by the side of the road suggested as much.

At the same time, living in Rwanda had clearly wrought changes on me. One trip back to Paris, I arrived late at night. I went to my friend's vacant apartment and slept. The next morning I tanked up on strong coffee and went out, losing no time in making up for living in a country without art museums, bound for the Louvre. Yet once there, I was unable to concentrate on the paintings, so stunned was I to find myself surrounded by scores of bleached people, rather than the normal chocolate brown that was the given in my world.

Later I realized I had come to accept other givens from Rwanda. In Annapolis, I remember being disapproving that the parents of a little girl who had died dedicated a tree at her elementary school to her memory. That was silly, I thought. Children died all the time. Why make such a fuss about it? When I arrived in Rwanda my cook/gardener Florien had two children. When I left two years later he also had two, only they weren't the same two: two had died and two had been born. Now, my Western sensibility returned, I am shocked at thinking of my own callousness.

Kigali

When the killing in Rwanda started, I caught myself thinking of what by my standards seemed the intrinsic violence of this world, something I'd seen in the trivial-in-context fact of a cat I'd had, and that I had to have killed.

Kigali is the name of Rwanda's sleepy little capital. It was also the name of a cat I had. I named her after the capital because I got her as a kitten from German friends who lived there. Hans was an engineer who ran the Deutsche Welle (Voice of Germany) Relay Station, and Peggy a fine-arts jeweler. They were evacuated at the last moment during the civil war by a Belgian military convoy on five minutes' notice, and later returned to Rwanda under the new regime.

I took Kigali back home in a huge borrowed pet carrier in the back of my Suzuki "Jeep," rattling over the rutted roads that led down from the hill where Peggy and Hans lived to the highway from where, looking back behind me, I could see the towers of the radio transmitters glowing in ribbons against the sudden dusk. She mewed all the way, the two hours back up to the hills by the volcanoes punctuated by starts of breathy terror from the tiny animal huddled in the corner of the oversized plastic box.

Once over her fright, however, she settled in well, learning to balance along the top edge of the banana-leaf fencing beyond which, in the distance, were visible the jagged tooth-edges of the chain of volcanoes. Sometimes she would miss her footing, walking along the balance beam of the fence with her white legs, incredibly long like a ballet dancer's, and teeter for a minute, wild-eyed, pulling back the leg that was over the edge and digging the other three claws into the crackling brown surface of the folded leaves. Her greatest pleasure seemed to be hunting the geckos that lodged in the banana thatching of the *paillotte*, the gazebo in the garden Florien had made where I had breakfast and did most of my work; frequently I would find her in a corner of the living room, batting at a tailless and enfeebled reptile that she would ultimately abandon when it was so near death as to have become uninteresting—or carrying one, squirming, from room to room in her mouth.

My shopping was done in Ruhengeri, the one-story town by the foot of the volcanoes that was filled, on market days, with hundreds of people wearing bright clothes and carrying baskets on their heads overflowing with potatoes and vegetables. Of course, there was no canned cat food for sale here. As far as that went, having a pet here in this country—especially a pet that was fed, rather than being left to forage for itself—was both an incredible luxury and an incredible waste. It was never without some feeling of bad conscience that I had my cook cut up the glistening red cubes of beef that were my solution to the problem of what to feed the cat—a solution arrived at after failed attempts to produce a cooked food involving rice and chicken—and dump them in her dish where she ate greedily, her sharp teeth exposed as the little knives they were and her eyes seeming to slit in sheer pleasure as she tore off great ungainly hunks and swallowed them in convulsive lunges.

The meat came from town as well, though from the slaughterhouse on the outskirts rather than from the shops in the center, near the post office. There was meat only three times a week, and this from only one animal a day-so that there was something almost personal about my participation in its death through my purchases of its flesh. The cow was killed—on the concrete slab that served as sales area and carving block—far earlier in the morning than I ever got up, so I never heard its lowing or saw the knife flash through its throat. I could only guess what must have happened here from the bloody pair of horns that were thrown to one side and still covered with flies by the time I arrived in my car, the metal wheelbarrow filled with the liquid sacs of innards, and the sides of flesh being hacked apart by the butcher, his apron discolored with old juices that formed a kind of lacy background to the fresher colors of that particular day.

By the time I arrived there were already a cluster of buyers on hand, to whom the butcher dispensed sections from the meat on the concrete after weighing it in an ancient pair of scales, or cut pieces of the trembling innards that seemed about to overflow from the wheelbarrow. My cook transacted the business for me while I sat and watched, arriving back at the car with the plastic bags we had brought full of solidity that was both smooth and pliant behind the outer skin of plastic, the meat still warm; from the sun or the body of the now hours-dead animal, I was never sure.

It was the public, almost shared fact of this larger animal's death that made the almost cruel pleasure of my cat in eating of its flesh less horrifying, made it seem less strange that a tiny feline could eat with such sharpness of teeth and evident enjoyment these near-cubes of bovine flesh cut by the knives of men. Wasn't this the same food that I ate, disguised by grinding and by sauces? Weren't we all linked in the same cycle of blood, the same circle of death that was, at the same time, a circle of life? Tennyson called Nature "red in tooth and claw." And we as part of her, I thought as—with all the contradictions of my over-refined Western sensibility—I chased the cat to take away from her yet another squirming gecko whose slow torture and death was meant to provide her amusement.

Afternoons in the Milles Collines

Kigali was the living being I was in a purely physical sense most intimate with, at least during my second year in Rwanda. For the first year, I had been sporadically involved with a beautiful Tutsi woman named Floriane, who I imagine is now dead. The relationship was based on mutual lust: we had eyed each other the first time we saw each other in front of the U.S. Embassy. She was gorgeous with her clothes on, and dazzling without them: as beautiful as a model but with fully formed hips and breasts that made my heart jump out of my chest when I looked at them, her skin a gorgeous deep chocolate brown. The situation was made complicated by the fact that Floriane was already living with an American man, not bad-looking, I thought, and evidently decent to her. She had to lie to him about "visiting her family" in order to come see me; several times I was unsure whether I had simply been stood up for the weekend, or whether the situation had become impossible for her. Without telephones I couldn't tell; the evening slated for her arrival lengthened and then was over several times. Each time it turned out, or she said it had turned out, that she couldn't make the fabrication hold.

We had trysts in the Hôtel des Milles Collines in Kigali, too, later the center of the radical Hutu radio station during the civil war. But soon Floriane began to fear that the desk clerk would recognize her and that word would get out, despite the fact that I got the room and she slipped up later to "visit" me. We made love in the sunlight of late afternoon filtered through sheer curtains, the air dusty with tiny motes dancing in the bars of light that fell on the bed.

I didn't know who was using whom more, she or I—though of course it was clear to me that she had more to lose. If both her American boyfriends—me plus the man she was living with—gave up on her, Floriane would have no protector and no link to the kind of life that she was used to living. She had studied something secretarial in Brussels under the protection of an older Belgian (to whom she gave sexual favors?); now she worked for the UN in Kigali. Ultimately my sense of being part of a chain of users and used overcame the force of my lust, and I began to tire of it all. And that summer, I met Martha again, and fell in love, in comparison to which even Floriane's exquisite body began to uninteresting.

Skinny legs

So I was left, that second year, with the cat, Kigali. When I stretched out my hand in the morning, it was Kigali's warm fur that I touched, her breathy meow that greeted me as I opened my eyes. With her skinny body that no amount of beef could fatten, she sought the warm crevasses of my body: groin, armpit, the fold between my legs. Yet for all of her affection, which I probably should have identified less sentimentally as her instinctive search for warmth and the smell of another living being, my stroking hand traveling across her body as she lay in my lap would sometimes seem to arouse in her instincts which I hadn't put there. She would squirm suddenly, bite my hand so that blood came, and go shooting across the room, sliding on the bamboo matting and yowling as she ran. I didn't hold it against her that she wanted to escape the burden of affection I was asking her to assume—if that's what was going on. Still, these abrupt knife-edge alterations were disconcerting, creating uncertainty on my part as to whether, at any particular moment, it would be Jekyll or Hyde that would be at home in my little cat. She must have been sired by a wild cat, perhaps one of the many once-domestic animals that expatriate Europeans let loose when they left, or foolishly gave to their servants along with money and injunctions to feed. But why should local people spend money and meat on animals, that God made free, or give them better food than they could afford to give their own children? Of course they let the animals go. And the lot of feral animals in Rwanda is nasty, brutish, and short.

It was one of my cook's duties to take care of the cat when I was gone, and to feed her in the morning before I got up. I never asked him what he thought of cutting up cattle to feed to cats; he'd seen enough Europeans come and go that he was tolerant of our ways, and I think he liked me. Indeed, he was almost gentle with Kigali, though she was not the type to rub against anyone save when she wanted food, and she ran from everyone including me except when I was sitting or lying down. I don't think it would ever have occurred to my cook to look for affection in an animal; he was a devoted father and husband, sensibly channeling his affections onto beings of his own kind. Yet the fact remained that the local people seemed, by our standards, almost gratuitously cruel to animals. Or was this simply being practical, unsentimental, the hard-headedness of our own farmer grandparents? I often wanted to cry out against the tiny boys, cow- or sheep-herders since an early age, whom I saw dragging along the roads an animal that hopped on three feet, while the rope was hooked to the fourth, by which they were pulled inexorably on, or the men who held up ducks or chickens bound by their feet and upside-down as my car passed them on the highway, or who thrust rabbits up by their ears.

Some months later I went away for the weekend. On returning, I discovered that Kigali had urinated in the middle of my bed. When I was over the shock and disgust, I reminded myself that I had heard of animals punishing their masters by urination for their absence. I was touched in some odd way: thinking that my presence meant so much to this strange wiry little creature that she would want to punish me for its withdrawal. Yet at the same time I was offended: to piss right in the middle of my bed! It was as if she had struck to the heart of our intimacy, a relationship carried out on the slabs of foam that padded my bed and the chairs in this house, and the only places where she had contact with my body.

Without comment, my cook washed the mattress and put it out to dry. Both of us thought that it had done so after a day in the direct tropical sun. Yet when I tried to sleep on it that night the weight of my body caused the wetness—that had, in fact, only retreated to the interior of the foam—to reach its edges once again, and I felt this secret wetness on my skin.

From that time on the bedroom door was closed when I went away. Yet Kigali would strike without warning, and seemingly without logic; clearly presence or absence was no longer the issue. I couldn't forbid her to sleep with me—she would yowl and scratch at the closed door until I gave in. As a result, I would occasionally get up from a night spent with her in the warm puffs of the comforter I'd brought from Germany, which we needed here in the central African highlands for protection against the cool nights, have her purr and meow in pleasure, and come back from the bathroom to find a soaking pool of yellow in the middle of the still-warm sheets. I tried punishing her, slapping her or pushing her nose in the urine; I tried forcing her to her box, or outdoors to make sure she was empty of urine. She ran squalling away from my slaps, and squatted unwillingly against the pressure of my hand in her box, withholding the drops I wanted to see in the sand.

My time in Rwanda was finally coming to an end. Clearly I couldn't leave her here to suffer the wildness and deprivation, the lice and attacks by animals that—I imagine—her probable progenitor had suffered. And after all, I was fond of her, in the way that we are fond of those who have been on the receiving end of our feelings. I'd made inquiries about how to take an animal on the Air France, figured out how to drug her so that she wouldn't yowl in her basket. I even found a travel basket at the market, with a lid that closed tightly, and I tried a few times to acclimate her to it—attempts that always ended by her turning into a squalling mess and clawing her way out of my arms.

I decided finally it made more sense to give her to another European who would take care of her than try and take her back to America, where I was to take on my job at Annapolis. The academic life I was going to, with its inevitable apartment living, had no place for an animal, and the logistical problems of returning with so much luggage, so many trunks, and a cat—even one knocked out with pills, as she would be—began to loom larger. I found a promised home for her, an American planter who had lived in Rwanda for thirty years, and who could be counted on to take good care of her, and let her be an outdoor cat—the solution, perhaps to her wildness.

I came back one day to find once again a drying pool of urine in the middle of my bed. I punished the cat; my cook once again washed the foam; I slept that night once again on the guest bed. The cat slept with me, cuddling against my leg, while I wept and ran my fingers through her fur. It was suddenly clear to me that I couldn't leave with a friend an animal that urinated on beds—especially since the friend's mattresses were not, like mine, of easily-washed foam, but instead great tickings of feathers on which she had slept for decades. As for my first plan of taking her with me, even if I could somehow integrate a cat into my life in America, what point would there be in taking back at great trouble and no little expense an animal that (despite my attempts to talk myself out of such feelings) insulted me and touched my most intimate habitation by polluting my bed?

I remember feeling that night a sense of bitterness at the unfairness of things that was deeper than any I had known in the years leading up to this point. What overwhelmed me was my utter inability to communicate with this creature, to explain to her that because she could not pee elsewhere, I would have to kill her. While she stretched and yawned and exposed her tummy to be rubbed, I cried. Why could love—there's no other name to give what I felt for this skinny animal—not allow us to communicate with the creature for whom we feel it? Finally, it was by subterfuge alone that I was able to get to sleep that night: I told myself that if Kigali didn't repeat her performance in the three or four weeks before my departure I would, despite the evidence, call her cured, and simply warn my friend not to leave her unattended in the bedroom. I left, so I told myself that night, the choice of life or death up to her. And so I slept, my fingers on the cat's soft side as it rose and fell.

The next day passed without incident, and the next and the next. And by the last week I had begun to think that this had been a single last, isolated incident. One afternoon, however, the pool was there again in the middle of my bed when I came back from classes. There was no point in punishing her; instead I hugged her to me, knowing now that she would have to die, and I would have to make the arrangements.

I'm sure that my cook would have been glad to strangle or drown the cat for me, had I only mentioned it to him. But I refused even to pursue this easy way out. If the cat was to die, I felt, it should be by the rules of the world which had shaped her life—which is to say, by a shot from a veterinarian—rather than by the rules of the world in which I had been a guest, and that I was in a sense contravening by having her as such a pampered pet.

With some inquiries, I found a veterinarian in Ruhengeri, a local doctor whose primary work was giving inoculations to cows. I visited him with three days left before my departure, and asked him if he could give a lethal shot to a cat. Of course, he said, standing in the door of the dark room with a big wooden table that was his office. He had a German product that did this, very lethal. I asked to see it, and was somehow consoled by the German lettering on the box that I traced with a finger: *Gift*, it said. Poison. The gift of death.

The next day, my jaw set with tension, feeling the horror of having the sun shining and the children playing (but what would I have happen on the day scheduled for the death of a cat? should heavens open?) I put Kigali in the basket that I had bought to take her back to America and, disregarding her yowls, bumped along the five miles to the village. The veterinarian was friendly, inviting me in and asking me to help hold her. Around her jaws he wrapped a dirty rag that an assistant picked up from a corner: they sometimes bite, he explained. He shaved the inside of one of her hind legs with a razor, carefully, exposing her pinkish- white skin and a meandering vein. For the needle, he said. I held down her head, the head that had both nuzzled and bit me, that had eaten cubes from cattle many times her size and tortured countless small reptiles. Perhaps the cat sensed my tension, or perhaps I was only holding her very tightly; she didn't move.

Then the veterinarian held the needle poised over her leg, a needle which he filled from the surgical bottle, puncturing the plastic cap. He stuck, and I felt my arms tighten. He couldn't find the vein, and stuck and stuck again into the bald area on which the vein stood out. Even then Kigali didn't move. Abruptly the man straightened up, explaining that he was having too hard a time because she was so thin, and that he was going to stick the needle directly into the her heart. And so it was with a great plunge and a sudden jerk that my cat abruptly ceased living there on the rough surface of that wooden table, the rag tied around her head, her heart full of *Gift*.

I paid the veterinarian, thanked him, and put the limp body into the basket where she had never wanted to stay; now she curled compliantly in the gentle curve of its webbing. By now I was crying, and hurried to get away from this man who must think me strange, over-sensitive, or outright ridiculous. And I jolted the five miles back to my house, the car now silent, the road dusty, the dead animal curled in the basket beside me.

I buried her in the back yard, in a towel she'd liked and that I had chosen the day before. In digging the hole I broke into a plastic pipe that ran, I imagine, from the toilet. Full of meditations on the intrusion of practicality into circumstances of great emotion, I patched the pipe, filled up the hole, and dug another hole. As I dug, I wept. And for what? For the hoary realization that the world goes on after the death of others, and will do so after one's own. For the need of great creatures like ourselves to love, and be loved, if only by small animals that bite us. For the necessity to choose among alternatives where life and death are only two options to be considered among many others, rather than absolutes. For the ridiculousness of my tears for one small cat in a country of people who suffer from so many diseases, in a world where so many things need more urgent attention than a household pet. But at the time, the realization was new to me that despite all of my efforts I too would be called upon to acknowledge my place in the circle of blood, new as well the thought that I could be guilty through doing something to which, nonetheless, there had been no alternative.

In 2004 I re-established contact with a former colleague at the University, a Rwandan Tutsi now working in Kigali. He himself had been out of the country during the 1994 massacres, but his wife and children had been killed. He had re-married, he told me, and had two children, and had taken in two orphans. He then listed other colleagues: this one killed, that one survived. One had even died "naturally"—the quotations marks were his.

What would that be like, to be unable to prevent the massacre one never saw coming of one's family? To be a plane-ride away in another world, unable to defend them, wondering if one had been irresponsible to leave them in the first place—and then to have to start again, to live in the place where it happened, with new people, a new wife, new children. . .

Life asks incredible things of us: to look up and have the sense of living another life, real enough in its own way but somehow precarious—

How far it takes those sorts of people away from the people who are still living their first life, indeed the only life they have ever known, and who do not have this sense of the fragility of all existence, of all plans, a sense of the vanity—as Samuel Johnson called it—of human wishes.

Five
LOVE, MARRIAGE, BABY CARRIAGE

In the summer between the two years I spent in Africa, Martha's and my relationship, until then platonic, took another turn.

We had been childhood friends, she my little blonde confidante in the third grade, always my friend through the teasing common in junior high, and worse in my case because I was a year younger than the other kids, wasn't athletic, and gave myself airs. We went through high school together, though she dated the football captain and was chosen for the Homecoming Court while I affected my long woolen scarves and hung out with the Bohemian set. We went our separate ways in college. Eventually she married a psychiatrist doing his residence and returned with him to Salisbury. I remember her wedding dress, and her wedding, in the church in Salisbury her grandfather had helped get off the ground. Her breasts swelled out of the top; one of them had a scarlet spot on them—nerves, she later told me—that confusingly enough made my heart beat faster.

I visited her occasionally while in Salisbury, saw first her tiny blonde daughter like a clone of herself, and then the second. She and her (for my taste) rather bland, preppy husband Tom came to my mother's house for dinner when I was there with their infant daughter in a car seat. Tom was a non-practicing Jew who ultimately converted to Christianity. Because he was marrying a *shiksa*, his parents, though apparently indifferent to their Judaism, would not come to his wedding. Sometimes I saw her only once or twice a year, but still there was no time when I was completely out of contact with her.

Apparently the marriage went from bad to worse, though I got only the faintest intimations of this from Martha. We sat on her couch in the suburban house she and Tom and bought and she listened: this even today is how I see Martha, listening. I only got the fill-in on their life when I was married to her, though I now realize that what she was telling me then was a sentence of death for our own marriage. Her second marriage paid the price for the first.

Martha told me that when she was married to Tom, she felt as if she had three children, not two children and a husband. Once I despised Tom for this. Martha and Tom's sex life was apparently close to non-existent, enough to produce two children and little more. Indeed local gossip suggested that at least towards the end Tom was going out with men, something I find all too conceivable now that I know just how much of an iceberg Martha could turn into when something displeased her. Who knows where we will look for comfort? It was only later that I reflected it took two to tango—or not; in the beginning of course it seemed to me that the whole travesty of her first marriage was Tom's fault. Whose fault was the travesty of her second?

After the two girls were born, Martha told me, Tom stayed out much of the night, and would come back at 3 a.m. to sleep on the downstairs couch. The most astonishing thing for me about all this was that, in order to avoid conflict, Martha never asked him about any of this. Her husband didn't come home until 3, and she said nothing! I found this unbelievable at the time: subsequently I came to understand that for Martha, tranquility, even if only that of a calm surface over a subterranean hurricane, is the greatest good. The one who raised his voice first lost the game. Confrontation was to be avoided at all costs.

Tom had never been particularly well-adjusted and became less so as the years went by. In the final years of his life, he was apparently on a drug high much of the time—I saw him giggling and free-associating. Legally blind, he looked at interlocutors out of the corner of his eyes, turning his head slightly off-center to involve his peripheral vision in the process of perception. The fact that he wore shorts in the dead of winter, kept the air conditioner down to 60, and set up fans all over the house suggests that there may well have been some sort of chemical imbalance in his system. It seems likely too, Martha later told me, that he suffered from bi-polar disorder, manic one moment, depressive the next.

Two years before Martha and I married, Tom killed himself with his own pills, alone in the empty house that he had refused to leave despite Martha's insistence that he do so. He apparently took several handfuls, replaced the cotton in the container, put it in a brown paper bag whose top he folded down, put the bag in the back of the cabinet under the sink, and, back in the bedroom, lay down on the bed to die. Tom also believed in pills for other people than himself. After his death his estate was sued for malpractice by a woman who had been given the highest dosage of a particular chemical ever known to have been prescribed.

I had gone to see her at her parents' house the Christmas of my first year in Rwanda. By then, Tom had been dead a year. I had always thought Martha something of an inscrutable Eternal Female, always willing to listen to problems, always kind and patient. That evening on her parents' porch, I saw another side of her, and it electrified me. It was warm, and I was wearing shorts. She said something about my "great legs." As a gesture of kidding affection between friends, this would have passed unnoticed. In the context of our painfully chaste relationship, her acknowledgment of my body, and so by extension of her own sexuality, touched me to the quick.

Strange, how so much can hang on so little, at least where the body is concerned, like the brief but electric vision Charles Bovary has of his future wife Emma greedily licking the last drops of curaçao from an upended glass. My feelings for Martha must have been building since Third Grade, an avalanche that only needed a tremor to start it. I remember one entire two-hour trip in my car along the twisting road to Kigali where I seemed to float, high on my own feelings. I sent Martha letters telling her what an effect she had had on me; her replies encouraged me. Even at this point I was somehow convinced that I was going back to the United States to marry her. It was meant to be: I had known her all my life. In my take on things, she was the victim, having been misused by her psychotic husband; I had enough love to heal her wounds. She had two beautiful little girls who needed a father, and whose father she had asked me to be. What could be more perfect? I was the man for the job, with all it took to take on the challenge. This re-crossing of the strands seemed to me a miracle, proof that it is never too late to go back and do something right.

There is a poem by Margaret Atwood called "Siren Song," which refurbishes the legend of the sirens by taking the point of view of one of the creatures herself, unwilling captive of her own mythically-determined island prison and of her "bird suit," as she calls her feathers, fated to sing to the mariners to whom she knows she is irresistible. She can draw these men in, but they can never save her or release her from her servitude, as they will always die precisely as a result of their attraction to her. The song? "Save me, save me." It gets them, as the siren observes, every time.

Martha, I thought, wanted me to save her. Or perhaps I wanted to think that she wanted me to save her. Now it seems to me that I was a prisoner not so much of her as of image of myself: I was a knight in shining armor, riding forth to rescue his lady love, a woman I had always idealized, now widowed and alone with two tiny clones of herself, a woman who said she wanted me to be a father to her children. How could I not gird my loins and rise to the challenge? I would, I vowed, be the best husband and father that ever was.

Certainly I was ready to hear, or imagine I heard, this siren song. I was hungry for obligations to others, having had so few for so long to anyone but myself. What obligations more instantaneous than the family represented by her two small, fatherless children? Teaching in Rwanda had felt like pouring water on the desert: I had bright students who could absorb all that I had to say, but because they had so little background, what I said functioned as discrete packets of information rather than, under more ideal conditions, part of a more general loam. It could never cause anything to grow. What I taught them was reflected back at me, but in exactly the form that it had gone in. No plants could grow from it; I was ready to garden.

Utterly and completely

I loved Martha utterly and completely. That first summer I'd stay up all night, making love to her for hours, my hard body seeming to have found its perfect complement in the soft hillocks of her rounded breasts and hips. Even in public, I wanted constantly to hold her hand, caress her neck, smell her hair. I lived for the touch of her skin and thought her the most beautiful woman in the world. Thus my agony when later it seemed as if a goddess was turning into a demon before my eyes, like the famous drawing of a young woman that, with a shift of perception, becomes a hag, or one of those Renaissance etchings of the worms crawling out from behind the rotted skull of a creature who, from the front, looks whole and healthy.

Knowing that my time in Africa was soon to be over, I looked for a job close to Salisbury, where Martha lived. One day I arrived in the office of the cultural attaché in Kigali to find a telegram waiting for me. The job at Annapolis was mine if I wanted it. I went out that night in Kigali and celebrated with friends. The next morning I left with my friend Arnaud and his sister for the Rwenzori, the Mountains of the Moon, where we climbed amid some of the world's most spectacular scenery, and dined on the tinned French food that Arnaud had brought along, including a bottle of good wine for every evening. (We three had a dozen porters.)

Leaving Rwanda for Annapolis seemed like an apotheosis, the achievement of all I had hoped for. It was moving toward unification with a woman whose presence had been a subliminal fact of my life since childhood, moving toward a job in a place that was familiar to me. It seemed to me that I was finally achieving order in a life that had been disordered, moving back to the center when I had been living on the periphery. And with no loss of time! I was even getting the children I would have had if I had married a decade before. Everything came out all right in the end; things turned out as they were meant to do. My *Wanderjahre* were over; now reality would begin.

I have to insist on the way things seemed to me then, because one of my later realizations was that all these perfect congruences, these apotheosis moments, ultimately unravel. If we could end the play just here, it would seem as if our life had form. Only we can't end the play here; we have to live on through the next act, and the next and the next and the next. It's one damn thing after the next.

U.S. Naval Academy chapel

Martha and I were married the summer of 1988 in the Naval Academy Chapel, after I had been teaching at Annapolis for a year. The wedding was beautiful; everybody said so. Keith, now dead from AIDS, played the 'cello; our family friend Norma, now dead from melanoma, sang. The little girls, Jane and Sally—as I'll call them—looked like angels in long salmon-colored dresses of watered silk Martha had made in Salisbury, wearing crowns of flowers in their hair. Martha made my heart thump by putting her hair up in a French twist because I had said I liked it that way. Keith was my best man, and Martha's sister was her matron of honor. I thought: This is what we've been aiming at all our lives! I could hardly breathe for sheer joy.

It was hot, and I remember the tiny beads of sweat on the back of Martha's neck. After a night near Middleburg, where I turned out to be gloriously wrong about being too drunk to perform sexually, we flew the next day to Paris. We drove, along with half of France, to the south that first day of August.

The big tragedy of the honeymoon, or so it seemed to Martha at the time, was that her camera was stolen out of the car in Aix-en-Provence—we were lucky more wasn't taken, it turned out, as the area was rife with thieves.

"All the pictures of our honeymoon!" she wailed.

In later years, I reflected, it didn't turn out to matter. So before having a reaction to a loss, we should wait to find out if it matters. Maybe in the long run it won't end up even being worth mourning.

We lived that fall in my bachelor apartment in Annapolis, tiny for four, while we waited for the unfinished house we'd bought to be habitable. Not that we spent the whole week in this apartment. Set apart from most people's habits by being the daughter of a multi-millionaire, Martha simply locked up her house in Salisbury and walked away from it rather than having to sell it in order to buy the next one. Since the apartment was small (and made smaller by having Martha defend Sally's "right" to leave her toys strewn all over the living room), we went every weekend to this house in Salisbury, where there was more room, and a yard. Besides, Martha didn't like using the communal laundry room in the basement of my apartment.

Every Friday afternoon we packed up the car and drove over the Chesapeake Bay and down the Eastern Shore. Within minutes of our arrival at her house, the children were across the street playing with their friends, and Martha was settled happily back in her previous life. On Sunday afternoon we simply turned the key in the lock again and cast the spell of slumber over the house until the following weekend, returning to the apartment in Annapolis, me to live, and she, it seemed, to count the days till the following Friday. Between taking the children to school and picking them up, she sat in the apartment apparently mourning the fact that she was not in the boring town I had lived to escape. Why couldn't she get out of the house? Volunteer? At least walk around? Why this infuriating passivity? She had, after all, agreed to come to Annapolis.

In November, we moved into our house, set on its plot of red earth that turned to hills of mud in the torrential rains we had that year. The house was, by my standards, huge, the lot palatial. When the agent first showed us the site and the plans of the unbuilt house, which would cost a quarter of a million dollars—a lot of money for the time, and money I didn't have—I felt as uncomfortable as if I had somehow been cajoled into the Monte Carlo casino by a bunch of high rollers.

"I can't afford this," I said. "I'm just an Assistant Professor at the Naval Academy. This is the kind of house you get when you're a Professor at Princeton."

Martha looked at me. I was ashamed that I made so little money, and said no more. As it happened, it turned out we could, after all, afford it: my father produced, surprisingly, a generous contribution. It seemed so quick, the transition from living in central Africa on a Fulbright Professor's restricted salary, with my worldly goods packable into a few crates, unsure of where my next job was coming from, to this sudden immersion in the material world. As a result of the sudden unexpected largesse from my father, I could hold up my side, and by extension my head, with this woman who could spend me blind and not even be aware that she had done so.

Martha made clear just what a piece of junk she thought the house was—this house that seemed to me so grandiose, so beyond my means. No hand-made lintels, she pointed out, unlike her house in Salisbury. All of it, she sniffed, was done on the cheap. Of course, she was right: "spec" houses nowadays are rarely made with loving care, and builders try routinely to go with the cheaper alternative.

Perhaps because Martha had functioned as a single parent even when Tom was alive, her world revolved around her children. Probably it would have done so anyway, as she never held a job. The situation even got worse after Tom's death, as Martha began to use Jane as her confidante, and routinely gave in to Sally out of a mixture of motherly indulgence and the need to "make up to her" her father's death. Sally ruled the roost; I assumed both Martha and I saw the need for that to stop. If Sally didn't get what she wanted immediately, she threw a fit; Martha always gave in and got her what it was she was throwing a fit about. Such fits were always front and center in the family; she was never given a "time out" or told that she could re-join the family when she was quiet. Instead, she had only to demand to have all eyes, except mine, on her. My eyes were always on Martha, trying to pry her away from the involvement with Sally that Sally so clearly wanted. Martha was horrified that I was trying to take her away from her child. Sally demanded access to Martha a half a dozen times a night; Martha saw nothing wrong in giving it to her. She bugged her great-grandmother mercilessly for some toy she thought she'd been promised, though the old lady was in her late 80s and frail; Martha thought this normal: "She's only a child," I heard a hundred times a day. Yes, but a child who had managed to make everything revolve around her.

Still, I loved their little hands in mine, their faces looking up at me. I loved the evening ritual of bath and story. I loved the most trivial family excursions, out to eat, to the park, to the zoo. On Valentine's Day, when I got Martha a dozen red roses, the little girls each got a red carnation in a vase. I assured them that "we" were all getting married as a family. I loved to hear them call me "Daddy." Yet I could see that I had my work cut out for me. I felt myself up to the task.

Sally ruined dinner after dinner, trip after trip, by demanding a new toy she absolutely had to have on pain of the earth ceasing to exist that, the following day after Martha had, inevitably, given in and bought it for her, would already be gathering dust in the cellar. Every day, I corrected Sally a dozen times for a dozen things that, had they been done, would have made living together possible. As psychiatrists subsequently made clear, the result was a pattern of constant nagging, which for Sally was a form of attention, for her the highest good. I can hear my weary repetition now: Don't track mud-laden shoes on the white carpet. Don't get out of your seat while we're eating dinner. Don't eat with your hands. Don't leave the front door wide open to let the air conditioning out. You don't need all the upstairs lights on to go to sleep. Put your toys away. Don't drop your dirty clothes on the bathroom floor: put them in the hamper. When I finally raised my voice, about the third or fourth repetition, Martha punished me for yelling by becoming upset and withholding sex. Sally learned to ignore me. All the while, Martha glowered at me and dripped bitter poison inside, developing severe stomach ulcers within months of our wedding.

It was a world where "no" was rarely said by anyone but me, and, when said, was interpreted, based on past experience with Martha, to mean "in a minute, when you've carried on a while longer." I tried and tried to convince Martha that she had to have a stronger backbone, or at least get out of the way and let me impose the limits. She merely looked at me: it was, after all, looking at me that I remembered Martha before. According to Martha, the reason I failed to be as sympathetic to Sally was that I wasn't her father, and had never had children. Again and again she interposed herself between me and the children: if I couldn't give Sally what she asked for, she, Martha, would do so. The possibility that it was in no one's best interests, least of all Sally's, to give her what she said she wanted, never seemed to occur to Martha, no matter how many different ways I tried to find to say it.

How little I knew her, after all. I now realize we can talk to, live with, even make love to another person and have no idea who that person is. So much the more so if that person herself has no idea who she is. And doesn't even know she doesn't. No wonder I am left cold by the easy black-and-white right/wrong "motivation is all" world of the Naval Academy, with its belief in an understandable world, absolute classifications of good and evil, honor and dishonor, and its assumption that people are who they say they are.

In this house I learned some things about Martha that I hadn't known. She didn't like men. She felt she had been manipulated by Tom. She simultaneously sought her father's approval and resented him for never involving her in the real estate business which he took over from his foster father. (Martha's father was orphaned at an early age and was raised by a childless, wealthy couple in town.) Had she been a boy, she said, she was sure that would have been running the business. Because she was a girl, her father overlooked her utterly. Her sister's first husband, being male, was taken immediately into the company. Once her sister left him for the man she was having an affair with, he was no longer in the son-in-law track, but still remained with the firm. Even the son-in-law, Martha said hotly, was given a real job.

I'm a tall man with a loud voice, two of the things that, she says, attracted her to me. Yet they also mean that by definition, my way of expressing myself was not be that of her whispery-voiced mother, nor of her own father who had far too tight control of his household ever to have to raise his own voice. And I have opinions about everything. When Martha allowed the children to watch junk television as if there were no tomorrow, the professor had to protest. When she allowed Sally to fill up on junk candy or soft drinks, I thought my responsibility as an instant father meant I had to object. When Martha played the radio and the television simultaneously to fill the void, just as her mother did at her own house in Salisbury, I asked her to turn them off.

She later insisted she felt attacked. Yet I couldn't just keep quiet, as she assumed and hoped I would. She had, after all, asked me to be the father of her children, which meant that I agreed to be responsible for them. Being responsible meant thinking about the consequences of actions, which clearly neither they nor she were doing. Thinking about consequences of actions meant trying to change those actions which were leading to bad results. This, I later learned, was thinking like a man. The problem was, as I later understood, that Martha saw nothing wrong with things as they were. I was creating the problem, not dealing with an extant one.

Later when the divorce came it turned out to be the easiest thing in the world to walk out and shut the door behind me, leaving two children well provided with money from other sources. At the time, I would have said I loved them. At least I told them this continuously, and tried to show I did. By the same token, I told their mother I loved her for much longer than the point at which it was probably true, so that when I was finally released from my self-imposed servitude, I realized that what had seemed so solid, my commitment, was in fact riddled with holes and crumbled from the emotional equivalent of dry rot.

I failed to impose order in my family, failed to make the proper place for Sally. After I left, she kicked over the traces, going through a troubled adolescence marked by substance abuse, promiscuous sex, and car accidents that totaled at least two cars. Over and over again during my married life, I pleaded with her mother to take a stitch then to save nine later on. Martha told me I was uncaring and unsympathetic. As a result, Sally later required not nine stitches, but ninety-nine. Or was it ninety-nine thousand?

Probably no one could have tamed Sally; I was a fool to think I could. The effect was like trying single-handedly trying to stop the spinning of a carousel that goes faster and faster by hanging onto the side, like the one that derails at the end of Hitchcock's *Strangers on a Train*. Still, my only shred of hope would have been to have Martha firmly on my side. Instead Martha became my enemy, leaving me trying to impose order single-handedly, in the name of a relationship that was itself being destroyed by my efforts.

I know that in the world as a whole the dominant force is chaos: the jungle takes over the abandoned house inside of days. I spend my life fighting against chaos: exercising so that my muscles stay hard, creating order out of the disorder of my students' minds, picking up things that need to be picked up, mowing the lawn, reading so as to keep down the cobwebs in my own head. All we can do is create small islands of order in a sea of chaos: it is our duty as human beings, this our Sysiphean task. What Martha wanted me to do was nothing. Precisely nothing: let Sally control the household, and let Martha deal with it, or not, as she saw fit. This was chaos, and the woman I loved was telling me to contribute to the chaos.

I didn't beget these children, I wanted to scream, and yet I'm willing to try to do the right thing by them, the thing that should have been done long ago. Thank me, admire me if you like. Instead, Martha came to hate me.

What drove me on? Why did I rise to the bait again and again, try to say, for the thousandth time, "no" to Sally and explain why to Martha? Why didn't I just throw big pieces of furniture? Hit somebody? Leave? I think this is the male burden: a feeling of responsibility. Somebody had to do this, and I was the one not only whom the Fates had elected, but the one who had volunteered. I wasn't giving up. If the kind of responsibility I felt, and the willingness to return again and again into the hail of bullets, isn't a positive thing, I have no reason to live. Yet I learned the hard way that being principled not only doesn't ensure success, it can ensure failure. No one will ever thank me for my efforts with Martha's children: not her, not them. Finally I had to admit myself beaten and walk away in order to save myself. It was a victory for chaos. Of course Martha reaped its bitter fruit, with the long years of psychiatric institutions for Sally, her ongoing problems, her slow recovery. Does Martha now regret her shackling me while Sally pulled over the whole edifice and I seethed in impotent fury? I don't even think she believes she was to blame.

Furniture

Our agreement when we moved into the house without the hand-made moldings that November was that she would move her furniture from Salisbury. Yet Christmas came and went, and no furniture had been moved. More puzzlingly yet, the same pattern of weekend immersion in Salisbury we had fallen into in the apartment continued.

"This isn't what we talked about doing," I said. "Why are we going to Salisbury?"

"I want to," she said.

I didn't push it, telling myself that having a wife and family just wasn't going to be like living as a bachelor.

We spent that first Christmas with her parents. I had imagined we might stay in our own home and found some traditions of our own. For her, it was simply a given that she and her sister, each with their second husbands, should dance attendance upon her parents in their huge pile of a house on the Wicomico River in Salisbury. Indeed, it turned out that all major holidays had to be spent with her mother. Her father stayed out of things. When we arrived, whether for a holiday or a visit, he was usually watching a golf tournament on the television, and continued to do so for most of the afternoon and evening, barely turning his head to acknowledge our presence.

I often thought in retrospect that I should simply have refused to go to all these holidays, as I should have refused to address her parents as "Dad" and "Mom": I had assumed I would call them Herman and Dot, and quickly learned that this was not what Martha had in mind. Yet in a strange way I think I was charmed by the very onerousness of giving in to someone not myself, I who had been answerable to no one for so long. I had to be a big boy and suck it up.

That first Christmas, gifts were exchanged in the huge living room that no one ever sat in, with the artificial designer tree and the piano no one played. Gold and pearl jewelry was trotted out for the children, over-priced style-less men's clothing for me, and expensive women's clothing for Martha and her sister. Before the gift-giving, the family, complete with its revolving-door sons-in-law, had gathered in the television room with the big fire and the view of the river. Yet no one was watching the fire. They were watching the huge television set on the side of the fireplace where a cable channel played a movie of a blazing fireplace to the background of endlessly repeating Christmas carols.

Martha's father, as it happened, was a graduate of the U.S. Naval Academy, so this was the one subject of conversation I could count on for getting through a difficult evening. Martha's mother never went further than high school, and grew up in a small town in the soybean fields called Snow Hill, only a few miles from Salisbury. Now dead of cancer, she was at the time always immaculately dressed, painfully thin—from dieting, not from cancer—and spent her time knocking around the huge house her husband built for her on the water and going out with him to the country club at night. He still ordered for her in restaurants and made all the household decisions. The price tag of that Christmas with all its designer-label conspicuous consumption was certainly many thousands of dollars. When I commented to Martha, somewhat shyly, on the amount of money that had changed hands in such a short period of time to so little apparent purpose, she didn't understand. "We go all out for Christmas," she informed me. And that was the end of the discussion.

Spring too came and went and Martha had not moved her furniture to our house, where my few pieces from the apartment sat against vast expanses of white walls. Nor would she talk about the fact that she hadn't moved. In fact, she never addressed the matter, and when I tried to bring it up, she changed the subject. If she wasn't talking about it, it seemed, it wasn't happening. We argued constantly about Sally and the way she held the family in thrall. Martha denied that there was any problem save the one I was creating by my protests. Every time I said something was wrong I ruptured the illusion that all was well.

I came to hate the house in Salisbury that allowed her the luxury of not committing to our life in Annapolis, and the financial power that made it possible. One Friday in June as Martha and the children were packing the car to leave (I had by then abandoned the practice of going with them every weekend), we were, as usual, arguing. Undoubtedly there was an immediate impetus for the argument, but the real point was her unwillingness to talk about the effect on our marriage of simply walking out each weekend, relegating me and the place we lived to sidelines while she carried on the center of her life in a house for which my resentment, by this time, had built to almost unbearable intensity.

Abruptly I couldn't stand it any more. "As far as I'm concerned," I told her, "you don't have to come back."

"Fine," she said, and left with the children, slamming the door behind her.

The marriage, I was sure, was over. Never one to shirk dealing with unpleasant consequences, I immediately put the house on the market. Yet after several weeks, we were seeing one another again, and after several months, sleeping together—though always, I later realized, under her roof in the house in Salisbury where she was mistress. By then it was summer. I wanted her to come back before fall. She refused, saying that she was going to stay in Salisbury for a year. Finally, after a year, at the last possible moment for school for the children, my family moved back, this time with furniture. Martha had put it off until the absolute last minute, but at least she had come. It felt as if victory had been snatched from the jaws of defeat. The unthinkable, an end to our marriage that I still insisted on thinking of as a storybook one, had after all been averted.

I had thought once before that our relationship was over, six months before we married. After a particularly knock-down, drag-out phone argument, I sat down and wrote her a letter saying that it was over. Without even getting this letter, Martha apparently sensed that it had been a more than usually serious altercation, and did something she had never done before: unannounced, she got in her car and drove the two hours to Annapolis, walking unannounced into my office at the Naval Academy. As she walked in the door, both of us burst into tears. I took from her gesture of driving into the void, a difficult thing for her, that she didn't want it to be over after all. Neither did I. We made love, and made up. I suppose things were never solid between us, though I told myself they were, taking each individual breaking through of the sun as the beginning of the new tomorrow.

Amnio

Three years passed. Things seemed to have calmed down with Sally—or at least seem to have done so in memory. And Martha finally became pregnant.

She came home from the hospital after a gall bladder operation, which had followed fast on her ulcers, announcing that she was no longer taking the pill; she became pregnant almost immediately. When she told me, my heart leapt, the words "Oh sweetheart" on my lips. For a moment, I tasted absolute happiness: I was about to have a child! Yet I never said the words. Martha turned away from me, her face hard: she was, I suddenly realized, not pleased. I remember the feeling of having to catch my exclamations of joy in mid-air and return them to safety, clamping my teeth tight to keep them inside. Within a matter of weeks, however, she had warmed to the idea of being pregnant, and gradually, as if testing the waters at each step, I allowed myself to feel the gratitude and joy I had wanted to feel from the beginning.

We went for amniocentesis: the chances of birth defects, most specifically Down syndrome, rise precipitously past 35; she was 38. To be sure, the doctor was not unduly worried about problems; my wife, as he put it, "got points" for having two healthy children already. Nonetheless she was anxious—largely about the test itself. When the day came I could see why: it involved having a long needle stuck into her stomach, and though the doctor could tell from the ultrasound screen that the sharp metal tip was nowhere near the tender fetus, the experience was still upsetting, not to mention painful. It went on longer than normal: the doctor had to attach several vials to the needle, and push it in again and again to get the flow going. I could see her getting pale; finally the same motion that pulled out the needle seemed to pull from her mouth the vomit that only narrowly, as she turned over, escaped ending up on the floor and made it to the waste basket instead.

Everything was fine. The news came in a phone call from the hospital analyzing the results. I could imagine the person on the telephone, saw in my mind's eye the place from which they were calling: we were the ones who took the brown paper bag with the vials to the hospital. For $60, the doctor told us, we could get the courier to take them, but we decided that I should take the day off from work and go to downtown Baltimore after the doctor's office. We would make an afternoon of it. After we dropped the vials off at the hospital, we would have lunch at an artsy bookstore and café on Mount Vernon Place in the old center of town.

When we found the lab—entering the building beside a vacant desk that clearly should have had a security guard—both of us were struck by how disorganized things seemed: located off a crowded hallway on one of the top floors, the hallway itself turned into a rudimentary obstacle course for the entirety of its length by refrigerators, boxes, and at one point a table with a half-eaten chocolate birthday cake. When we entered the room whose metal plate bore a number we had been told to look for, the research assistants looked at us somewhat uncertainly, as if people were not supposed to come in at all. Finally we told a woman what we wanted. We were reassured when she seemed to know what we were talking about.

We were reassured too that they wanted our insurance number; somehow it made things feel more legitimate. Yet our sense of the inherent disorganization of the operation grew yet stronger after the first phone call. Hello, a voice said. This is University Hospital. Is this Martha? Yes, my wife said. We have good news, said the voice, it's a boy and perfectly fine. Oh, said my wife, getting excited. We're so glad. Both of us wanted a boy. We have two girls already.

The voice congratulated my wife. Then it grew businesslike. According to its records, it went on, you wanted to know the sex of the baby, but your husband did not. Was that right? My wife was surprised, and somewhat confused. No, she said. Both of us wanted to know. The voice was taken aback. Is this Martha XX, it asked? naming a last name not ours.

Martha almost began to weep from frustration and anger. No, she said. And how did you get my number? If you've gotten my number confused with some other Martha how do I know you didn't get the tests confused too?

The voice had no answer, and hung up. The next day we were still waiting; in the days that followed several voices called to tell us that, that though the mistake was regrettable, there could have been no mix-up on the tests: the other Martha had another test entirely. They were very sorry for the error of phone numbers, which they could not explain.

In the brouhaha, our real results, conveyed by another voice that seemed to have no inkling of the problems caused by its earlier cousin, came as something of an anti-climax: in this preview of coming attractios the baby was still healthy, but now it was a girl. When my wife mentioned the first mistake they insisted; no mistake this time. Healthy, and a girl. And it seemed that one phantom voice had conjured up one reality, only to be replaced by the reality conjured up by another phantom. This is the one that corresponded, they said, to the bulge in my wife's stomach: the child who came out would be female.

In the Doll House

I was still thinking of our girl-child to be when, a few weeks after the test results, I went with Martha to a store in a small town north of Baltimore that sold doll houses, along with their furnishings—miniature versions of everything necessary to stock an upper middle-class house from 1970, 1920, 1900, or 1880; further back than this the collective history of doll houses does not seem to reach. She wanted to get one for Jane, the older daughter who seemed so the model child she was almost eclipsed in the arguments over Sally. I had seen miniature rooms before, inset into the walls of the Field Museum in Chicago, and in grosser versions in the bedrooms of little girls of my acquaintance. Yet I had never before been in a shop that sold the constituents of these fantasies, a place that made possible the construction—in exchange for not inconsiderable amounts of money—of such a thing one's self.

The town where this shop was located was itself a miniature and rapidly gentrifying scale model of the towns and cities in which I spend most of my life. Located within a half hour of Baltimore's center and just off the north-south superhighway to southern Pennsylvania, this town had in the years shortly before become—what with urban expansion and the extending suburbs—just close enough to the city for shoppers to find attractive the brief trip out across the rolling hills on the weekend. The result was a string of newly spruced up houses-turned-into-shops down what had recently been a tiny decaying main street; a new coat of paint on the local Methodist church; and a convenience store or two in a cluster by the gas station—where the city dwellers tanked up at country prices before returning home or bought a quart of milk that would not yet be warm by the time they were once again within reach of their refrigerators—as well as this shop intended for other people than for the residents of this town rotten behind its face-lift, set in an old house made in any case unusable for normal purposes by the newer hardware store whose parking lot surrounded it.

It was high shopping time that week before Christmas—dolls and doll houses being linked to our holiday fantasies, perhaps as a remnant of the Victorian age which has cast its images over our visions of December celebrations. The rooms of this shop were crowded with Junior-league type mothers shepherding sub-teen daughters, or buying for themselves. (The objects sold here were too fragile for real children, as well as being too expensive: not the functional plastic dolls of three-year olds, but the dream-toys of adults.) The rooms were crowded too with merchandise, shelves and shelves full of tiny couches, wicker chairs, china, chandeliers, minuscule loaves of bread (these last for the Victorian table) and even—for the kitchen of the last quarter of our century—miniature spray bottles of window cleaner.

Many objects were displayed *in situ,* like smaller versions of real furniture stores that invite the prospective buyer to think of this one corner of the huge partitioned floor as her bedroom, this other one as the designer bath; by leaning closer to the glass front of a cabinet the viewer imagined him- or herself in the overstuffed warmth of a nineteenth-century living room, the cool white tiles of a 1920s kitchen. Others—those pieces that might otherwise get lost—hung in plastic bags: the tiny blob of plastic fried eggs, the diminutive plastic candles that could not be burned, even the mop and bucket that had been spilled into a pool of its own congealed water.

Everywhere one looked there were tiny worlds that could be entered at a gaze, many furnished with Christmas trees decorated with infinitesimal Nutcrackers and strings of red pin-heads standing for cranberries. To be sure, in the case of some objects the gross reality of the human world intruded. For though the chairs on the Edwardian dining room could be made tiny, the weave of the cloth that made up their cushions could not be, and the viewer imagined the discomfort to tiny rumps of the oversized warp and woof of the cloth, the effort necessary to shift minuscule buttocks against the pull of such giant threads. The puddles of varnish at the bases of the newel posts were such as would be made by human-sized brushes, no matter how small. And the oriental carpet (made in Belgium, the tag on the back said in letters that would be two feet to those who would walk on it) gave up all pretense at weave and simply presented its pattern in paint on the square of cloth.

How comforting it was to think that, should there exist such tiny creatures as could live in doll houses, they would not only inhabit dwellings like ours, but show a historical development parallel to our own—their own doll's Victorian age giving way to miniature Maxfield Parrishes, and from this to the one-inch shopping bag overflowing with Wonder Bread and Wheaties. How inevitable the course of Western history becomes, how right and proper, if even a race of elves lives— seemingly by the force of inevitable development—its own identical, miniaturized version of the same! But we don't have to go to "The Doll's House" to have this sense of valorization in the miniature. The attempt to redeem our life by repeating it in smaller versions drives all art and powers all organized thought, not to mention filling most of the rest of our waking hours. Our stories of people's lives that can be read in a single evening, our arcs of recognition and betrayal that fill only ninety minutes in a movie theater, our meaningful situations tucked into magazines that sketch a whole character in a few pages: what else are these but slightly more abstracted versions of the four-inch-high chairs? What else too are our systems of philosophy but the miniaturization and hence deformation of structures so vast that we can never hope to sense them in their natural size? We're grateful to artists and thinkers because, for a brief moment, we taste the illusion that our own lives have a pattern and a purpose—and this because these people have seen them from far away, as if from an airplane, and given us their vision of the motions of the ants that in fact are the people below.

And children. Before Martha became pregnant and I knew I was going to be a father, I often wondered how it was that the vast majority of people seem to do very well without the structuring in art that to me seems as necessary as air—a means of rendering solid the otherwise inconceivable fluidity of life as lived. Sometimes, like Thomas Mann's Tonio Kröger, I envy the kind of people who never crack a book, who regard museums as tourist attractions, and who never enter a theater, asking myself if they have found a solution to the puzzling situation of being alive that I have not. That day in "The Doll's House" I realized that no one is free of the need for the frail comforts of conceptualization. For many people, I realized, putting 2 and 2 together, this sense of valorizing miniaturization is sensed in children, whose tiny hands, ears, and feet seem so touching and so beautiful: when a new creature comes from the womb and hence from nothingness, it looks like us! I too thought: I'm going to be reproduced! The nature of the miracle became clear.

And for those without children, it comes from the brief lives of household pets that we see grow to adulthood, then lose their hearing, become incontinent, and die. Or it's sensed in the confines of terraria or house plants, where leaves and roots in pots carry on their briefer, more narrow lives on window sills. How pointless it would seem to have a tortoise—that would live through several of our own frail lifetimes—as a pet, have a garden so large we had no idea where it began or ended, be lords of a realm so vast we could never chart it. Yet at the same time, it's only because of the existence of the wicker furniture of the doll's house, the tiny shopping bag of brown plastic, the pot of diminutive tulips—as well as the fingers of babies, the deaths of goldfish—that we can feel, however briefly, that we too are saved from the vast chaos of the universe on which float our tiny, fragile islands of order.

I thought that Alexandra was going to save me from chaos. If only I had known.

Six
THE UNRAVELING

Memento mori

Keith died that February, just before Alexandra was born. In fact, in the semi-delusional state he was in for almost the last year of his life, I'm not sure he even registered that Martha and I were going to have a baby, or if he did register it, that he cared.

When I would go into his room at the hospital during the period of his illness, I would usually find him asleep. When I woke him by running my fingers along the dry skin of his arm, he would open his eyes. Seeing him in bed was not, of itself, disconcerting: he had been horizontal for many months, first on the couch in his own house, then on the pull-out bed this contained, then in my mother's house, and finally here. One day, however, he was in a new position. I came in and saw him slumped over into his lap, the bones at the top of his back and into his neck exposed like those of a plucked chicken. When I turned my head upside down to look into his face, I saw that his eyes were open. The visit took place like this, with my head upside down as if lying on my back, and his gaze on his knees.

During these visits, some fragments of his consciousness would be closer to the surface than others. During one visit he remembered the name of the wife of a friend I had forgotten, but confused a sound from the hallway with the sound of his own computer, now hundreds of miles away. He could make a fist for the nurse and turn his head to the light when she asked him to, but at the same time insisted that he had bought for himself the bouquet of purple flowers on the sill. At one point he observed, as if for my information, that he was going to be in the other room the next time I came. What other room? I asked, and from his puzzled look—puzzled that I was puzzled, not from a dawning understanding that something was wrong—understood that in his mind's eye he was at my mother's house, in the period when he could get up from the couch in the living room to go in the bedroom for the night.

In this condition there was no sign of his mordant sense of humor, none of his irreverent politically-so-incorrect-they're-hilarious jokes, nor could he be in the kitchen whipping up a batch of sinfully caloric chocolate thingies or a heart-attackon-a-dessert-plate cheesecake, none of the things that had made people willing to put up with the hurts they suffered from him, caused by his unconcern with people's feelings, his procrastination, and his downright jerkiness.

After a certain point, I no longer knew what sank in and what didn't; I simply talked, telling the same stories over and over in the hope he would tell me I was repeating myself. He never did, limiting himself to nodding. Words were rare, and when they came, mostly beside the point. The doctor gave him an anti-dementia drug, my mother told me: this was why, as of a certain point, he no longer got the wild-eyed stare that so disconcerted me a few weeks before.

He was, in any case, spared some of the more aesthetically unpleasant possible effects of AIDS: blindness, blackening of the skin. My brother's end seemed more abstract than this, negative in nature rather than positive, extreme weakness and a fragmentation of the mind. As he went through phases, so did I. For example, I was embarrassed for a long while about his lapses of memory. I felt like the hostess who has to cover up the bad manners of the guest and keep the conversation going when, for example, he informed me that my father was out in the hallway, walking around, when I knew him to be elsewhere, or when he betrayed his utter ignorance of where he was. Yet even this inconsistency wasn't consistent: he had periods of what seemed relative lucidity, so I didn't know which particular phase we were in at any given moment.

Perhaps I was most embarrassed when he thought he was back in his own house. For, though he didn't know it, the house he imagined no longer existed: my mother had already spent months throwing out accumulated trash and giving things away, readying the house for the day when it would be turned back to the landlord in order to start long-overdue renovations. She wasn't being over-hasty in starting the clean-out while Keith lay in the hospital; he hadn't lived in this house for six months, and we all knew this was the end. The doctor wasn't willing any longer to send tubes down Keith's throat to clip away fragments of his lungs to see which particular kind of pneumonia it was he had: the discomfort of the probing wouldn't be worth it, the doctor said. Instead, he merely prescribed the treatment for that kind of pneumonia most common to AIDS patients. The problem was, the treatment was itself ultimately lethal, so that they decided to allow the medicine to drip into Keith for a limited time and then stop, hoping for the best. In any case the best would be measured at most in months, more likely in weeks.

For a time my brother's home was the hospital in Salisbury, a hundred miles away from Washington, where he lived. Nonetheless it was strange to think that he thought—to the extent that he did think—that his house still existed as he left it. Or rather, because he never spoke of it, perhaps had no reason to think the opposite. All of us have presuppositions that remain unchallenged simply because it doesn't occur to us that they could be otherwise: that the earth won't sink under our feet when we step on it, that a friendly face with an outstretched hand is not plotting our death, that our house will be there as we left it when we come back in the evening. In each of these cases, and in so many others, we can be in for a surprise.

In that countdown to spring, what unsettled me most was the feeling I had that many of the loose ends had been wrapped up, and that now all we were waiting for was the end—waiting, that is, for my brother to die. That last fall he was still able to peel himself off the couch to be taken out to Sunday brunch, when he ate and ate, as if translating all of his desires and contacts with the world into the single sensation of taste.

Along about November he was no longer able to walk to the car and we passed into the all too brief period of the home-cooked meals: I would leave my own family in Annapolis and drive to Washington to make Sunday brunch or lunch for us in the kitchen. Keith would eat with the plate on his chest, unwilling even then to lift his head and unable to come to the table. By Christmas he could no longer be left for longer than a day or two, and, increasingly recalcitrant, was talked into going to my mother's house "for the weekend," a weekend that lasted until a few days before his death.

At some level he had to have understand the progression in which he was engaged: was this why he never asked when he was going back to his own house? Finally he even stopped grilling my mother regarding the whereabouts of his car.

It wasn't only his own house he never mentioned; he was also unwilling to say anything at all about what was happening to him, or how he felt about it. Instead, it seemed that we were supposed to pretend that we simply didn't notice anything amiss. And this was a conspiracy of silence orchestrated by him, the logical outgrowth of his way of dealing with life.

Keith had always been uncommunicative, exploding into temper tantrums when his actions were questioned, and facing down disapproval with clenched jaw and fiery eyes as if daring people to object. A lot of what he did was objectionable. Keith was irresponsible, and he was hurtful. Perhaps silence was as close as he could get to the approval that was denied him. I learned early on to stay out of his way, and then went on my own.

Allowing myself to be controlled by him—or perhaps, simply seeing no point in not being so—I said nothing about his illness or impending death. For all either he or I said about the reason he was in the hospital, he might be simply taking an afternoon nap in this somewhat noisy, white-walled building at the end of my car ride. What was strange to me about this silence regarding his condition was that he himself seemed to feel no need to tie up loose ends, even conceptually. What was happening with his house? Who was driving his car? Where would he be buried? He never asked. Was he simply beyond caring? He didn't even refer to the fact that his end was near. Was he beyond caring about this too?

Sometimes I thought he might not be as unconscious of this silence as he seemed to be. Perhaps he thought the single brief conversation we had had two years before was all that was necessary. He was in the hospital, having been admitted with a persistent cough and weakness: this is when he was diagnosed as HIV-positive. At the same time he was told he had two years to live. For me—and I think even less for him—the sero-positivity itself was no surprise. His sexual orientation had been long ago digested by all in our family save my father, whom hadn't been given the chance to, neither Keith nor I having ever told him. Even Keith's bar-hopping lifestyle was no secret, at least not to Mother and me. I had been afraid it would lead to this end. What was a shock was only the small amount of time: two years. The doctor was very close to being right. When Keith died he had had two months extra.

His first hospital visit was when I did my crying: part of this conversation was a brief reconciliation scene when I spoke of the very different paths the two of us had taken, the way he had lived that seemed so strange to me, the fact that we had never been able to communicate. He told me he loved me. I told him I loved him. Feeling the need to at least have referred to the subject of death, I said I had no idea what awaited us at our passing. Keith dismissed this with a flick of his hand, and the subject was closed.

And then he was out of the hospital, in a brief reprieve during which he led a normal life—until he began once again to slow. During this entire time, not a word was said about AIDS, or death, or even his symptoms: no discussion of his dizziness, no acknowledgment of the fact that he was finally spending all his time on the couch, no mention of his weakened state that daily grew more and more blatant.

This conspiracy of silence had seemed marginally less bizarre when Keith was in his own home, or even in the bedroom in my mother's house. But in the hospital it seemed very strange indeed: could I speak to him of the hospital, the nurses, the tubes in his arm? Or were these things not happening either? What of his lapses of memory, his fantasies? How to hide these? And when, in his confusion, he thought he was back in his own home, I began to despair. His bicycle had been given away, most of the furniture had been sold or donated, and the record collection, vast as it was, had because of its extraordinary quality found a home at the Library of Congress. So frail, I thought, the life of one human being that holds together the structures of inanimate objects which, at his or her disappearance, break apart and fragment into new configurations, scattering across the earth to new owners whose possessions will themselves one day be scattered, or simply thrown away.

My mother preserved her composure during the process of dismantling, for the second time, the downstairs sex room. Keith had reconstituted it without comment after the first sacking. Not by nature hysterical, she seemed to understand, at least intellectually, the things to which human beings can be driven in slavery to their bodies. There must in addition have been some sort of maternal force at work that I can't begin to fathom: the same impulse as that which leads mothers to clean up the mess made by a baby, to hide its shame from the world, making her go into this room and remove its contents from the house in the trunk of her car. The same impulse had led her to bail him out financially, which she had done so often I'm sure Keith took for granted that she would always do it: he would blow the money he got from playing jobs on yet more records, yet another leather jacket, as if there were no tomorrow. For him, there wasn't. Maybe he was counting on that. Keith always looked the other way in a restaurant when the check came, and never even thanked the other person for picking it up. The February before he died I thought he was ignoring the check in a big way. I was most angry that he left us to grieve while he retreated into his silence, into the scrambled morass of his perceptions and memory which, if not precisely comforting, at least shielded him from any necessity to come to terms with what was happening to him.

His final victory over us, and the world, was the silence he had demanded from us: giving in to his imperious pressure, we didn't rage, question, or disapprove. Instead, we talked in terms of medications, of days and weeks, of incontinence and of safety alerts, turning the emotional to the merely rational.

During the chastened year following his initial diagnosis as sero-positive, as if in the attempt to go back and do everything again, he led what for my own norms was a model life: returned to the research on Gregorian chant that he had abandoned ten years before, played the 'cello more seriously, and seemed to stay home from the bars more. The upstairs of his house was once again filled with light falling on his houseplants and on his beloved cat (that outlived him by more than a decade), and filled with the inevitable voice of Maria Callas from one of his thousands of rare vinyl records.

For this brief period of his Indian Summer, he became what we would have had him be all along—at least in his upstairs life. Not, to be sure, more communicative, not more open about his feelings, not more immediately lovable—but at least, on the surface, organized, responsible, shepherding his talents rather than squandering them. A brief reprieve, as it turned out, and as such indicative of nothing at all—the less so in that the room in the basement, his downstairs life, come back in all its black-leather mirrored splendor during just this time, to be left for my mother finally to take apart once more. Did he ever think, I wondered as I sat at his bedside, of the fact that my mother would be the one to dismantle this room? Or was it as untouched in his memory as the rest of his house, by then virtually a vacant shell?

Fire escape

My marriage ended, I later realized, on a fire escape at the Naval Academy one rainy January day. The moment where Sally reached her apogee on these steps, when her spirited ascent slowed, crested, and then changed shape and form was the last moment of possibility for Martha and me. From then on it was all downhill. Past this point, the gyroscope spun out of control.

Two weeks before, Martha and I had gone to the Caribbean on a kind of second honeymoon. It was also a sort of celebration: our rocky marriage seemed finally on firmer ground. Alexandra was six months old. Furthermore, I had, finally (the hesitation was Martha's, not mine) adopted the two girls two weeks before Alexandra's birth. My lawyer later told me this was the dumbest thing I ever did. The adoption itself was my idea, too, I note ruefully: I didn't want any second-class citizens in the family. I knew the right thing, I thought, and I would do it. It ended up with no clear benefits and a huge price-tag. So much for doing the right thing.

The week on St. Barth's cost us $4,000, which we split, since I couldn't afford it alone. For that matter, I couldn't really afford it even halved, on the salary of a newly-promoted Associate Professor. Ashamed of how little I earned, though my wife knew exactly what that was, I said nothing. Martha was used to having what she wanted. On St. Barth's we slept late, tried to swim in the chilly Caribbean, ate wildly expensive meals, and made love. I did all the driving, as I had done on our honeymoon in metropolitan France. (St. Barth's is part of Guadaloupe, a French overseas department.) St. Barth's is hilly; I remember the road as an endless curve, the vacation as one great down-shift.

Despite all of what for me were drawbacks and the negative feelings I had simply swallowed, the time together was bonding; we felt like a couple again. We celebrated our renewed marriage in the San Juan airport on the way back by toasting with a beer. We should have saved the toast, though perhaps not: we would never have given it. We arrived home from St. Barth's to find that Sally had, in the words of a psychiatrist later, "taken control of the situation."

My mother was staying with the three children. After the first day, Sally had begun to complain of stomach pains. My mother had at first ignored them. After a day or two, she took Sally to the doctor, who agreed there was nothing physically wrong and suggested that Sally should simply be encouraged to go on with her life. This Sally refused to do. By the time we arrived home, she had been flat on her back on the couch for two days clutching her stomach and moaning with pain. She had not gone to school all week. My mother was being skeptical and largely unsympathetic; knowing there was nothing we could do and not wanting to ruin our vacation, she had decided not to call us.

Martha's first action was to fly to the couch and cover Sally with kisses and sympathy. Sally's response was to groan louder and beweep her fate with an unsympathetic grandmother. Finally, her mother was home. Things were going to go back to normal; the fountains of empathy could flow full out again.

The next day Martha herself came down with the flu, and stayed in bed for three days. It was intermittently rainy, but to get the children and myself out of the house, I suggested we simply go to the Naval Academy and take a walk. I was pushing Alexandra in the stroller; Jane was running along the path by the water. For a time, the sun poked out from between the clouds. For a few minutes, I saw Sally revive, her stomach trouble forgotten, running and jumping with her sister. She talked normally, having other things on her mind than herself, and seemed almost normal.

Abruptly the sun disappeared, and I felt the first drops of another shower. Sally had charged up the fire escape. I called her back, yelling that we would have to go home. It was in this moment, like the nadir of the yo-yo's trajectory when it stands still before changing direction, that Sally recollected herself. Her pains abruptly returned. It was an almost-normal child who ascended the staircase and a child spiraling out of control again who descended. Coming down meant going home, which meant home to the couch, home to her mother's sympathy on which she fed, home to a world that included a new father who said "no" to her when her mother said "yes." Inside of a few days, Sally was hospitalized. Her mother was convinced she had stomach cancer. She didn't.

Martha and I always took separate spring vacations, since my Naval Academy spring break week never coincided with the children's school vacation. Martha and the girls had gotten into the pattern of going to Florida to see her parents, and duly left that year as well. A few weeks later, following our usual pattern, I went to Berlin. Martha, I later learned, never forgave me for being gone when she took made "the most difficult decision" of her life, Sally clinging to her and weeping. I had deserted her in her hour of need. It had been clear to me for months that Sally would have to be committed, even though I could not convince Martha of this. I knew that if I were around to insist on or make the decision, Martha would blame it on me. My days of insisting, at any rate, were over. Martha alone had to make the decision, or she would forever feel that I had forced her into it, and resent me. The way things worked out, she got to resent me even more.

The night before I left for Berlin, Martha took me out to dinner and was very sweet. I assumed this meant she was comfortable with my going: in fact it turned out, as she later explained, that she was trying to be so nice I would realize that my responsibility lay with her, and cancel the next day's trip. But of course, had I stayed, what she wanted was that I, though by now legally the father of the child, should leave all decisions up to her and not interfere. I imagine it's one of those gender things, where women hope that men will figure out what it is they want and give it to them. It entered my head even less to cancel my own vacation in that Martha never altered her own vacation plans for me, not even to cancel her trip to Florida to stay for my brother's funeral. I had told her to go, and meant it: staying wouldn't bring Keith back. What point was there in making everybody sad? So Martha had Sally committed, and made it my fault.

When I returned, I began daily visits to the hospital to see Sally. A few days later, she had her say, spewing hatred in a stream uninterrupted by the young, inexperienced psychiatrist, making it clear that I was the cause of all her troubles. Martha later admitted that Sally was "speaking for" her. Sally announced that she would kill herself if she was made to return to a household that included me. By this time she knew that her biological father had killed himself, and knew what an effect this would have on Martha. I think of the hatred contorting Sally's features that day when in the psychiatric ward (the first of three hospitals, as it turned out) the bitterness fairly spewed from her lips and she denounced me as the source of all her troubles while my wife sat in silent agreement, the daughter in the institution speaking for the mother outside of it. It reminded me of engravings from the Middle Ages of scaly demons escaping the mouths of the possessed as the priest waves the crucifix at them: I have heard the equivalent of such demons. Or her suicide threats in the hospital, as bone-chilling as they were ridiculous: when she put her hands around her own throat and threatened to strangle herself if she was released to a house that contained me. Such an unerring instinct for hurt, I thought, such an iron will, such an incredible willingness to play the game of getting one's way with even the highest stakes.

Some of Sally's problems were biological, it turned out; at least the doctors said so, and began a program of treatment that will apparently continue all her life. In her moments of dementia, Sally's face, Martha told me, made grimaces she had not seen since Tom made them. Yet Sally does not remember him.

Separation anxiety

Part of the diagnosis for Sally was something the psychiatrists called "separation anxiety," by which they meant that Sally had never developed a personality separate from Martha, as well as obsessive/compulsive disorder, and several other things. In a sense, then, I was vindicated: the hours I had spent explaining why Martha should not allow Sally to dominate our lives through her fits, her naggings for a thousand objects that, once procured, were quickly forgotten, her demand for immediate access to my wife even in our most intimate moments, had been proven correct. But at what price? My articulation of what was happening itself became hateful to my wife, raised to believe that rocking the boat was the worst evil, and that bad things don't exist until you articulate them. I told her again and again that she was killing the messenger, punishing me for saying things that ought to be clear to her. That made her punish me more. I too became more desperate, more strident, feeling the marriage I had so badly wanted to save crumbling under the weight of my attempts to save it. If I didn't fight, I'd lost. If I did fight, I'd lost: Scylla and Charybdis.

If I tried to explain this to my students, told daily that if they are "motivated" enough they will succeed, how they would look at me!

The day after Sally's self-exorcism that blamed me for everything, Martha insisted she and I drive separate cars to visit Sally. What now, I wondered? The same incompetent young psychiatrist sat us down for a "family conference" in the absurdly small chairs of the schoolroom in the psychiatric ward, its modular walls decorated with the artificially cheerful primary-color cut-outs of elementary schools.

"I understand you have something to say, Mrs. Fleming," she said pleasantly.

"Yes," said Martha, her eyes flaming and her jaw set. "I want a divorce and [turning to me for the first time] I want you to move out."

First the daughter lets loose, then the mother, I thought. "Anyone else care to take a shot?" I asked, laughing a mirthless laugh.

I refused to go. Sally could not, for her own sake, be allowed this victory, even though Martha was demanding it with fire in her eye. Give a nine-year-old the proof that she has the power to make or break a marriage? How could Martha even be asking this? The joke turned out to be on me: Sally did, of course, have the power to make or break our marriage. Besides, it didn't turn out to be worth saving, something that these events themselves made clear even to me—to whom this one conclusion had hitherto been forbidden. I had the sensation, again and again, of hanging from the window ledge with the tips of my fingers and having the person I assumed had come to help stomp on my hands. How much pain can I bear? And why am I doing it? Yet ultimately, I know, I should be grateful to this child who, I at one time thought, had ruined my life, for in fact she saved it: she got me out of a ruined marriage that I would never have been able to allow myself to leave.

The horrors of my marriage were not those of the newspapers: no one was ever beaten, no one had an affair, no one had a double life. We celebrated holidays together; I picked the kids up from school, brought my wife flowers on our anniversary and played footsie with her under the restaurant table. And not least horrible of all the fact that the marriage contained enough love and good faith that it kept me coming back again and again for more punishment, like being kept just alive enough by the torturers that one is aware of one's pain Echoing Wilfred Owen, I want to say: was it for this that corn grew tall?

Kitchen sink

Because of insurance strictures, Sally could only stay in the first hospital for two weeks. She was, therefore, moved to a second hospital. The first hospital had been, as she insisted, her "home," the children there "the only ones who had ever understood her." In fact, she had vowed never to leave at all. Because of her suicide threats, she was transported to the other hospital in an ambulance.

But Sally didn't take to the second hospital at all in the way she had taken to the first. Like a piece of tape that sticks well the first time and, removed and re-stuck, less well the second, she failed to bond. Inside of a week she was asking her mother what she would have to do to come home. "Do what the doctors tell you," Martha said, clearly taken aback by Sally's ability to control herself if she wanted to—but still failing to draw any conclusions. Overnight Sally became a model patient.

We celebrated a rather chilly Easter with Sally at the beginning of the second week, on the hospital grounds, with baskets and candy. The second hospital's program, like that of the first, was based on pills and behavior modification, not talk with the patient. Sally was in fact eager to talk, to express herself. The psychiatrists were surely right in saying that letting her talk was only making her worse. I can never forget her free-associative, ranting tirades in the pre-hospital days she lay on the couch clutching her stomach that would go on for hours, punctuated only by screaming and crying. Inside the psychiatric ward, by contrast, she was allowed only a few minutes at a time to say what she had to say. Her behavior was charted on sheets that listed desired actions: gets up, eats without prodding, greets parents, is respectful to doctors, and so on. For each of these miniature blocks of action patterns she would, upon successful completion, receive a star. A certain number of stars entitled her to privileges.

In the middle of the second week, abruptly having become a model patient in order to gain what she wanted, Sally came home. For a few weeks she was perfect: grateful to be out of the hospital, cooperative, smiling, and acting very, very carefully. .

Soon things began, ever so slowly, to unravel. The old, perhaps "real" Sally began to peek through the façade: she would refuse, for a moment, to do what she was asked to do, before recollecting herself and pasting on the smile, be just a little slower than she should have been on the uptake, or a shade surlier than the charts—continued at home—called for. This was not merely because no child, not even a "normal" one, can be cheerful all the time: the veneer of cooperation began to mar noticeably as the threat of the hospital grew ever further away.

Hong Kong

Back then, in these now-distant days of my first life, I persisted in believing, despite all evidence, that problems were solvable. I reasoned that our time had been taken up with Sally, had revolved around her completely: now it was time to get on with other things. I had applied again for a fellowship to teach for a year at the University of Hong Kong. In fact, I had been offered it the year before, and had turned it down because of Martha's many fears related to the fact that Alexandra would have been only a few months old. Knowing Martha's fear of the unknown—even Annapolis was alien to her, and that was only 90 miles from Salisbury, "home"—I gave up quickly, after trying to convince her that Hong Kong had hospitals too, and nannies who came considerably cheaper than in the States. The second time I was offered it was after Sally's re-assertion of control. Martha refused again. I tried to persuade her: if it doesn't work, you and the girls can come home. The fellowship came with private school tuition, so there was even a financial advantage: the immediate saving of $20,000, for me at that time a huge amount of money.

The friends I announced it to thought it was a fantastic idea. "How exciting!" they said.

Not Martha. So far from home! In a strange country! Full of foreigners! She also decided that I had been trying to manipulate her by not discussing with her the fact that I'd re-applied: I was trying to blackmail her with a fait accompli, force her to do something against her will. She wasn't going to be forced. Her face grew hard. I apply for a lot of fellowships, I said. What point was there in re-discussing this one until I knew if there was anything to discuss? Anyway, I applied for it last year and you knew about it then.

Yes, she said, but she thought the threat had gone away. The threat! I said. Not the opportunity, the chance: the world outside as a vast menace, something horrible against which she had to defend herself by burrowing deeper into her hole.

We had just gotten through a difficult period with Sally, she said: we weren't going anywhere. That was the point, I said. We've spent all these months dealing with Sally's problems. What about me? I'm being sacrificed to Sally.

Martha set her jaw. I could do as I liked.

My choice, then, was this: go, doing something I had been angling to do for many years, or stay with my little girl. Even if I came back at Christmas, she wouldn't know me. And wasn't this the most important time of life to bond with a child? Forced to choose between my child and what I wanted to do professionally, I turned the fellowship down, for the second time. It nearly killed me, most of all because of the sense that Sally and Martha had the power to determine my life by the sheer weight of doing nothing, like a great black hole into which the universe could be dropped without a sound, a hole that would remain gaping and take in another universe a moment later.

The fellowship people were disgusted: they just knew something like this was going to happen, given that I had turned them down last year. They had offered it to me again despite their better judgment that suggested to them I was simply unreliable. I gnashed my teeth. Yet that afternoon, after hanging up the phone, I pushed Alexandra on the swings, telling her uncomprehending little face in baby-talk sing-song: "Not going to leave you. No, not going to leave you." As it turned out, given who Alexandra became, it might not have mattered if I had left for a year, or even two or three.

Hands

I moved out of the house for good one day in June. I had told Sally not to wash her play-dirtied hands in the kitchen sink over the dishes that were usually there waiting to be rinsed. Besides, the bathroom was right next door, with a sink meant for just that purpose. Yet Sally preferred the kitchen. The result was that, each time, I had to tell her to wash her hands in the bathroom sink, and each time it was as if I had just that minute invented the rule; each incident took at least three repetitions before she huffed and puffed and stormed away to the bathroom, usually dripping her hands purposely over the linoleum, while Martha looked away. The psychiatrists later pointed out that we were in a destructive cycle: Sally had nothing to gain by internalizing the rules; her goal was interaction with adults, even negative interaction. And as I later understood, Martha hated me for correcting Sally, and was rooting for me to fail.

This particular day in June the front door slammed, Sally ran down the hallway, and in a minute was at the kitchen sink, full of dishes, with a soft plastic baby dish of Alexandra on the top.

"Go to the bathroom to wash your hands," I said for what must have been the hundredth time under similar circumstances, counting to three before I did so, in as neutral a tone of voice as I could muster.

"But Da-ad," Sally said, and continued to wash her hands.

"Go to the bathroom to wash your hands," I repeated, louder but checking myself to make sure I wasn't yelling.

This time, Sally simply ignored me, intent on what she was up to. By now she had reached under the sink and hauled out a spray bottle of cleansing agent that I knew to be, if not mortally poisonous, at least not something that people, especially babies, should be ingesting, even in trace elements. In an instant she was energetically spraying it over her mud-caked hands, and hence liberally onto Alexandra's porous-plastic baby dish on top of the pile.

"Go to the bathroom to wash your hands," I said, abruptly turning up the intensity of my voice and sharpening the tone. Forces of protection for Alexandra stronger than any rationality were welling up in me, not to mention anger that Sally did what she damn well pleased despite what I said.

It was at this moment that Martha opened her mouth. "There's nothing wrong with her washing her hands there," she said.

I'll always remember this moment, because it was in this instant that the mists parted, things that I had seen blurrily suddenly leapt into clear focus. Martha had given me permission to leave this hell-hole. If the person for whom I was sacrificing my peace of mind, my tranquility, my very life, corrected me in front of the child I was trying to bring in line not only for her own sake, but for ours, then the contract was canceled. In this simple phrase, Martha had ended my servitude. I was free to go.

And so I did go, to the only other place I could go: my mother's house in Salisbury.

Still, thinking of the effect on Alexandra, I didn't want the marriage to be over. I called the next day and offered to return. Martha's response was, "I think it would be better if you didn't come back." She said later she thought I meant, come back from Salisbury only to get my things, which I had said I would need to do in the note I had left when I walked out, and sleep on the couch. But to me it was permission reiterated. I was no longer responsible for her or her children. And we would simply have to deal with the effects on Alexandra. Three days later, with my parents' financial help, I bought a house.

Yet once again unable to accept the finality of it all, this proof of broken dreams and shattered illusions, I began talking to Martha again, even talking of the possibility of getting back together again. It seems ridiculous now, but perhaps it was good that I tried even past the point of rationality: at least I now know that there was nothing left to give.

With the passage of time, I came to see that impulses like this were merely the effect of the machinery refusing to quit. More than a year later, Martha called me and wanted to sleep with me: I accepted, as a sop to my male pride. Little did I know that this session would legally erase in the eyes of the law all the time we had spent separated, and that the first question her lawyer would ask her would be, when did you last sleep together? Was this why she did it?

Finally even I was willing to accept that our divorce was inevitable. The unthinkable had happened: our romance was over, my childhood sweetheart lost to me forever.

Bleak House

Both of us agreed to a no-fault divorce.

My lawyer, Rob, had explained to me that my options regarding Alexandra were three. First, I could let Martha have custody of her. This I rejected immediately. She was my daughter, and I was going to help raise her. Besides, I had seen Martha's mothering techniques with two other children.

Second, I could try to get full custody myself. There were several things wrong with this option. I didn't know how I could take care of her all by myself. Anyway, I wasn't trying to take her away from Martha, whom I figured she needed. In fact, as my lawyer was clear, I might not win, and then I'd have nothing at all. In conservative Maryland, the woman still held the upper hand. Martha didn't work, and could spend more time with Alexandra. Besides, the acrimony that this option would produce was such that whether or not I won, Alexandra would clearly be the loser.

Little though I liked a lifetime of having to deal with Martha, the best, the only option for Alexandra was the third, joint custody. And to this, Martha had agreed.

Her lawyer wrote the initial proposal. Rob summed it up for me with a rueful shake of his head: "Bruce," he said, "they want money."

"They want *what*?" I said.

"Sure," he said with a grin. "The most usual thing in the world."

If someone had told me a year before that Martha, the daughter of a multi-millionaire who had kept my savings close to zero through my attempt to keep up with her, would end up demanding money from me, I would have laughed out loud. Me, a badly-paid academic who made me pant behind her spending more than I thought wise? Who made me feel wretched that I couldn't shower on her the diamonds and pearls her family thought proper birthday and Christmas presents? At that point, I had no sense of her greed, or rather her anger at me that was expressed in the desire to make me pay. She wasn't out for revenge, she later insisted: she just didn't know what her lawyer was up to. The scary part is, I almost believe her: as incredibly irresponsible as that sounds, that was vintage Martha. Deny all consequences of your actions, live moment to moment. Somebody else is always responsible.

According to her lawyer, she had a "lifestyle" to support: the private school for the children, though we had bought the house we did because of the excellent public schools, the country club she belonged to because the people at the Naval Academy pool weren't "her kind of people," the cleaning lady who earned as much as my disposable income, though I had offered to clean the house as I had been doing in my own. If your father is a multi-millionaire and your girlfriends have cleaning ladies and belong to country clubs, of course you too have to do the same. And of course, you hand the bill to the husband, or the ex-husband, as the case may be.

Discussion of her demands, it turned out, was not her lawyer's style. Why discuss when you can bludgeon and blackmail? And this in what was supposed to be a no-fault divorce that would allow amicable parenting of a small child! His first moves was to schedule a "deposition," a "discovery hearing": a time when, the clock of course running for him to collect his fees (a large multiple of my own hourly salary), he would "examine" my financial records from the past ten years to find out how much he could ask for. In practice, my lawyer assured me, we might be able to resolve the issues before this happened. Her lawyer, unsurprisingly, preferred discussion under the gun, with only one side holding the gun. At no point did it appear to have occurred to anyone that where co-parenting of a child is concerned, the feelings of both parties can't be destroyed without impacting the child. It's as if he were working with a completely imbecilic economic model, one that left a price tag off the most precious commodity of all: goodwill.

Being served

I received word of this deposition by being served with a subpoena by a frizzy-haired woman who rang my doorbell one afternoon.

"Yes?" I said, opening the door.

"Are you Bruce Fleming?" she asked.

Rob, of course, had told me about the whole wretched mechanism. "But don't worry," he assured me. "Lawyers send those things to each other. You don't ever have to get involved."

What, then, was this woman doing on my doorstep? I felt as if I had entered a horror film, still refusing to believe that Martha would sink this low, or rather, be a party to something so common, so hatefully run-of-the-mill. "You take that back and give it back to your slimy boss," I told the woman. "He's supposed to be sending those things to my lawyer, not to me."

For a moment she appeared uncertain. "Mr. Nositch said that your lawyer refused service," she said, her voice crescendoing from a waver to a compensatory over-aggressiveness.

"That's a lie," I informed her.

"That's what he said," she insisted.

Suddenly the whole thing seemed too tawdry to be borne for an instant longer. "Oh for God's said," I said, "Just give it to me," and slammed the door in her face as hard as I could. Though it made me feel better, I know it was petty: this woman probably counted herself lucky to get a job as a secretary to a weasel lawyer, one of whose requirements was delivering subpoenas to unsuspecting people on her way home.

Subpoenas! Discovery hearings! I felt as if I had entered an alterative universe. My lawyer could of course invade Martha's privacy with a subpoena for more "discovery hearings" right back, counter-suing for divorce from our direction and hauling her in for a "deposition." But how horrible: two wrongs didn't make this one right. Nor would I sink this low, even if she did. There had never been financial secrets between Martha and me. At least, not from my side. She knew exactly what I earned. I, by contrast, had spent years pointedly not asking Martha how much money she had or how much she might one day have, in order to make it perfectly clear that this was beneath us, and that our human relationship was based on other sorts of things: that I had not married her for her future millions or her current comfortable financial state.

I can hear with perfect clarity the sneers of this hired thug, the posturing, the swaggering, that day of the threatened deposition in his "chambers." No one had ever spoken to me the way this man did that day; I hope I reach my grave before another ever does: I'm not sure I could stand it a second time.

The most horrible thing was, this hired thug was using my tiny daughter as a hostage. Rob had made it clear to me that getting joint custody presupposed agreement on money issues, as no judge in Maryland would award joint custody to a couple who were unable to get along at least to this extent. Nositch, therefore, had only to demand the max, and threaten me with retaliation if I did not give in. Did he know I would protect Alexandra? I don't think he cared. Either way, he won: in fact, he won bigger if I allowed my sense of justice and my testosterone to rise to the challenge. In that case, I would be handing him what was surely his dearest wish: an expensive custody fight, where he would be able to submit a bill for many lovely hours of destruction. Saving the keystone of the agreement, namely joint custody of Alexandra, presupposed taking a beating.

After making me wait for over an hour, that day in his "chambers," during which Rob went back and forth, Nositch himself pushed into the conference room wearing an open-necked polo shirt. (I was dressed in a three-piece suit.) At least I had to assume it was he. Who else would be slithering about so openly? He looked at me contemptuously, then barked, as his first lines: "How much money do you have in the bank?"

Despite the tension of the situation, I was bemused. Do such slimy creatures really exist? I wondered.

Since he had not introduced himself, I figured he should. "Who are you?" I asked.

For a moment he was nonplused. "Fine," he said unconvincingly, his impetus broken for an instant. I smiled inwardly at his misunderstanding of the question. He was right, I didn't care how he was at all.

"I said, 'Who are you?'" I repeated.

He looked at me scornfully.

I smiled.

I paid for this opening victory.

He asserted the most outlandish things with a sarcastic tone of voice and a flip of his head. The older children "needed" to go to their private school, so the $20,000 Martha got from Social Security couldn't be counted as support. The children "needed" to stay in their four-bedroom house and would be traumatized by moving. Martha was "needed" at home and so could not work, even though I would have Alexandra half the week and she could hire a baby-sitter like all working mothers.

All of these arguments were plausible. The only problem was, they weren't true. This, I learned, is what lawyers do: they assert possibilities with all the force of fact, hoping they can get somebody to accept them merely because they are being asserted.

It was clear that Nositch's technique of choice for getting what he wanted was blackmail. First, there was the threat of beginning that infuriating invasion of privacy to which I would not be a party, the "discovery" hearings. "If you don't want to play ball," Nositch said countless times with a sneer, "we can just start these proceedings right here and now."

"Calm down, Ron," Rob would say, and we would begin again.

Then came the ultimate betrayal in a marriage that had left little, I thought, to further betray. Since Martha always came to a point, sooner usually rather than later, when she refused to talk to me or listen to me, on more than one occasion I did what seemed perfectly natural to me and perfectly unnatural to her, who could barely write a thank-you note without agonizing over it for hours: I picked up the pen and wrote a letter, explaining how I saw things and why I had reacted as I did. I had forgotten I had ever written them; she had laid them aside against a rainy day. I saw those letters again that dreadful day when, sneering in my face, her lawyer informed me that he could get me to do anything he wanted, since all he had to do for me to lose was show those letters to a judge. They clearly showed that I was a manipulative bully: if not, where were her responses?

I will never forgive the woman I had once loved, for giving into the hands of her hired strong-arm man my impassioned last-ditch attempts to communicate at her when she had shut up shop and withdrawn into a lump of frozen rejection on her side of the bed. Rob took a look at them and shook his head. "Bruce," he said, "I wish you hadn't written those." (A lesson: never write anything down.) How did she think we could possibly get along after this? Or did she think that I too, like Tom, would simply disappear or die, leaving her mistress of the hill?

I had brought that day in my briefcase, which I put under my chair, a talismanic copy of Dickens' *Bleak House*, that so-clear warning of what happens to people when they deliver themselves into the hands of lawyers. Occasionally I would touch it with my foot. At every turn I reminded myself that I could hit back and play the wretched game her lawyer was so eager to entice me into. Or I could downplay, damage control, and take the hits for my daughter, whom no one else, it seemed, was protecting but me. Please, St. Peter, I want to say now, tell me you noticed.

Finally after many hours Martha appeared, looking drugged, and allowed the thuggish Nositch to speak for her, letting him deflect all direct challenges on my part or attempts to speak to her directly. She was the princess who had to be defended against the ogre: I was not to be allowed to get at her.

Wrong script

This day in her lawyer's "chambers" was not without its comic angle, clear to me even as I sat in agony for my daughter. I had the feeling that someone had gotten hold of the wrong script. Excuse me, I wanted to say. Yoo-hoo, hello? The sock-it-to-the-bastard one's tomorrow. This one's the amicable split among people who always acted independently with respect to money, the velvet divorce that will allow us to raise Alexandra and somehow continue to communicate.

I'm now willing to believe—against all probability—that Martha never understood that joint custody presupposed agreement on monetary matters, either because her thug didn't explain it to her or she didn't take it in, wouldn't have been capable of thinking rationally if she had, or was so firmly convinced of the necessity of making me pay that she just didn't care. As so often before, Martha probably just didn't understand the effects of her actions, and this simply because she didn't want to. What chance had rationality against this stubborn blankness?

"I'm not doing this," she told me again on the phone. "My lawyer is."

"Yes," I said. "Your employee. You're paying him to do this to us."

To this she had no response. I wonder if she ever understood that she remained responsible, that human beings, as Sartre would point out, can never give up their freedom, even if they are letting someone else settle their scores for them. Sally, now Nositch: Martha was good at having others speak for her. In her mind that let her off the hook. If there is a theological defense of not guilty by reason of moral vacuity, Martha may get into heaven after all.

It ended by my giving her some money. Not so much that it crippled me, and not so much as she asked for (I refused to be the second husband to bankroll her lifestyle through a life insurance policy), but enough that she could feel that her principle was being upheld, the principle being that *the husband pays*. Part of my savings, which she had done nothing to earn and everything to spend. In return she "gave up" claims to my small pension and to alimony. I wasn't impressed: in my universe run by morality rather than legality, she never had a claim to those to begin with, so I couldn't be too impressed at her simply not compounding her moral turpitude by demanding them.

Rob assured me that the money she got was peanuts. That she should get any money at all from my salary horrified me, she whose actions had very nearly made it impossible for me to concentrate on my work at all, and who had clearly won the race to outspend me years before. The thought of her being rewarded for her actions and those of her lawyer appalled me. "Look at it this way," Rob said to me over lunch afterwards. "You give her money; in exchange you get your daughter and no hassle. You're buying peace and quiet."

"Yes," I said. "But it isn't justice."

"Bruce," he said, leaning over the table, "lesson number one is, there *is* no justice."

I know, of course, that sessions like this one are minor evils on the Earth, and nothing at all when compared to really serious things like torturers cutting pieces from their victims' bodies in dank cells, children locked in closets, or animals killed for the amusement of idle humans. In such a world, my own little temporary hell surely doesn't even register. Still, I felt as if I should run from this man's office screaming at passers-by, "Do you know what goes on in there?"

I imagine many of them do. I feel like the child who learns about sex for the first time and simply refuses to believe that everybody he sees has been engaged in such revolting actions. If I find intolerable something as quotidian as being served with a subpoena and being roughed up emotionally in a case that ended in a no-fault uncontested divorce and that never even came to a deposition, I will, perhaps, have led a sheltered life.

I'll never see our marriage Martha's way. And she, I'm sure, will never see it mine. Still, I can exercise my imagination. It must have seemed to her that a great wind had swept into her life and was mercilessly uprooting every frail sapling of her existence. Martha's assumption was that things were fine before, so any changes I demanded were piled on a scale and held to my account. My view was that, like someone occupying a bench all by herself, she should have moved over and left half of it to me: changes would have been written into the process of accommodating things to another partner, the other half of the marriage relationship. Because she never cleared off half the bench, everything I did seemed pushy, aggressive. What is it *now*? she must have thought. He's at it *again*. To me, it felt as if she was trying to shut me out of any influence in the marriage, consigning me once again to the very marginality I had sought to escape by marrying her.

"But you were so *dogmatic* about it," she said time and time again after we separated, when we were making the rounds of the inevitable "counselors." "If only you'd said, this is what I *think*, not, this is the way things *are*."

She must have felt so attacked, with this forceful male saying things so contrary to her world-view. Eat this, watch that, don't eat this, do this. At least he could have had the decency not to try and back up his claims with proofs, or with evidence; or to express them in objective terms. At least he could have expressed them as subjective expressions of feelings, rather than as perception of fact, so she could brush them off with a good conscience.

Martha, I later thought, had adopted half of a 1950s gender paradigm, the half that was advantageous to her. That the woman should be supported by the man: that was the part she liked fine. She forgot that the other side of that Faustian bargain had always been that the woman was obedient to the man: this she never tried to be; this I never asked her to be. She did things her way.

Duck in Box

While all this was going on, all the good in my life was centered on Alexandra, living, as she did for more than a decade, half the week with me. I lived for the feel of her soft hands on my face, the smell of her hair.

But Alexandra, it turned out, had problems. By the time she was 2 ½, it was clear that she was not talking at the level she should. Alexandra had some problems making eye contact, wanted to do the same thing over and over, and had to have what verbal commands she understood always in the same form. Many basic questions or commands, however, she simply didn't appear to understand. In response she would smile. Initially we thought it was because I was speaking to her in French, in an effort to raise her as bi-lingual: children raised hearing two languages apparently experience initial delays in speaking either, but when they do speak, speak both simultaneously. Gradually, however, both Martha and I began to think that other things might be at work, and, the divorce battle momentarily in a lull, we took Alexandra for tests in Baltimore. Some moments one remembers all one's life: for me, one will certainly be when we sat down with the doctors to hear the results.

What I heard was that "the wiring in Alexandra's brain wasn't hooked up properly." She was autistic, which then was diagnosed as PDD-NOS, even more frightening spelled out than as a string of letters: Pervasive Developmental Disorder, Not Otherwise Specified. Having decided that any cause was ruled out (forceps birth, mother on drugs), this "diagnosis of exclusion" was what was left: it described what she did. Pervasive Developmental Disorder. She could count to thirty, but did so over and over when she should be responding to something else, or said the alphabet every time invariably, from start to finish, without being able to break off or start in the middle. She was attracted to any absolutely predictable string of sounds. She read license plates with great alacrity, but words meant nothing to her, nor was it clear that she understood the concept of numbers: twoness, or three of something. More than a decade later, doctors tend to speak of Asperger's Syndrome, and see children like Alexandra as one of a wave of high-functioning autistic children who sprouted during the 1990s for reasons no one can explain. One theory, discredited in most circles, involves mercury poisoning from vaccinations.

The doctors told us to some degree what awaited us, but said we had done the right thing by intervening early: children can be shown coping mechanisms with early intervention, though their brains cannot be "cured." They told us she would have social problems all her life, being unable to pick up the cues that others pick up naturally, that she would have to be taught to speak rather than merely being left to pick it up by osmosis like a normal child, and that she would always have trouble with abstraction. Autistic children, we were told, see the trees but not the forest. And another tree is always another tree: generalization is difficult. And oh yes: "She won't do well on the SAT," one doctor said of my three-year-old.

And so began the wearying process of manually "patching over" what her brain didn't naturally do. Initially, Martha and I alternated in taking her to a speech therapist. The speech therapist was based near Baltimore, but saw Annapolis patients in an orthodontist's waiting room closer to town. Fate was surely laughing sardonically at this: the waiting room was the very place where Martha and I had gone for Lamaze class when she was pregnant with Alexandra, in happier times (this orthodontist is clearly a particularly enterprising one). Twice a week, for months, I sat a few feet from Martha, yoked to her forever to the woman I despised by the child I loved, who played with the therapist's toys on the table between us. Never anything in unadulterated form, it seems: never love without hatred. I sometimes wished a bomb would simply put us out of our misery.

The therapy was as much behavior therapy as it was lessons in speech. Alexandra's problem was not primarily forming sounds, but in understanding that language can be useful.

"Other children pick up these things by listening," said the therapist. "For Alexandra, adult speech is like an undifferentiated flow of water that just goes off her back. You have to slow it down for her to get it."

We said the same phrases over and over, in telegraph English. The therapist put the duck in the box. "Duck in box," she said. "Say."

"Duck in box," said Alexandra. "Say."

The therapist took the duck out of the box. "Duck out of box," she said. This time she left off "say."

So did Alexandra. "Duck out of box," said Alexandra.

"Give me the duck," the therapist said. Alexandra complied. "Give Mommy the duck," the therapist said. Alexandra hesitated. The therapist took her hand, holding the duck, and guided it to Martha. "Hooray!" she said. "You gave Mommy the duck!" Alexandra, pleased with herself, clapped her hands.

"Say," insisted the therapist, "I gave Mommy the duck."

"Say, I gave Mommy the duck," said Alexandra.

"I gave Mommy the duck," said the therapist.

"I gave Mommy the duck," said Alexandra.

"She imitates," I said. "Does she understand?"

"At least she's saying the right thing," the therapist said. "That's the best you can hope for at this point."

At least, this was the way the sessions went when Alexandra was in a good mood. Otherwise I found that I had driven forty minutes in traffic (the office was convenient to the house I lived in with Martha but on the other side of town for me) with a child I had to wake up from a nap and who refused to co-operate during the half-hour sessions or do anything other than wail.

At home, she repeated, without seeming to understand that she must take part in conversation. "Give me the ball," I would say. "Give me the ball," she would respond, and gave me the ball. "I'm giving YOU the ball," I would say, taking her part. "Giving YOU the ball," she would repeat.

In everything she said correctly I tasted the sweat of a hundred repetitions: "What is your name?" I asked her repeatedly. Then I give her the response: "My name is Alexandra." The first several dozen times, she would only repeat: "What is your name?" or follow it immediately by the answer: "What is your name? My name is Alexandra," as if she thought it a two-part litany for the same person.

Then abruptly, one day, she got it right. "What is your name?" I asked her. "My name is Alexandra," she told me. How we jumped and clapped.

By a certain point she was doing pretty well with describing the present. "What are you doing?" I would ask her.

"I'm eating dinner," she would tell me.

She was, too. "Good girl," I would say.

But time designations other than the present were unreachable. If it wasn't happening right then, she couldn't express it. Yesterday was gone, and an hour from now was not yet. If it wasn't the eternal present, it didn't exist for her.

Nor, apparently, could she understand the simplest contravention to her expectations. One day that summer we had gotten on our bathing suits to walk to the neighborhood pool, which she loved, only to find it closed because of a filter problem. The door was locked, and the pool was deserted.

"Door locked," I told her.

She cried.

"No one here," I said.

She cried.

"Come on," I said. "I'll show you."

We walked to the chain-link fence and looked at the empty pool.

"Go swimming?" asked Alexandra.

"No swimming," I said. "People all gone."

All she could do was cry.

One day, some weeks later, we had a success experience while swimming: she followed my pointing finger and tracked an airplane across the sky. "Airplane," she said.

"Yes," I agreed jubilantly, "airplane."

After the pool closed for the season, she still wanted to go each day at the appointed time. How to explain to her that the season was over? So one day we went for a walk and looked in the chain link fence. The pool had been drained. "Empty," I said. "All done."

I expected her to cry. She didn't. "Empty," she suddenly agreed. I nearly wept: it felt like the moment of comprehension in *The Miracle Worker*, where Helen Keller understands that "wa" means the sensation of wetness on her hands. I held her on my lap when she cried, and told her a thousand times a day I loved her. "I love you, Daddy," she finally said back. Perhaps she was only being a parrot, but she was my parrot.

Elmo or Ernie?

To teach her a sense of choice, I learned to hold out two fists: "Do you want Elmo or Ernie?" I asked, referring to her two toothbrushes with those characters on them. She imitated my gesture. At first she repeated. "Elmo or Ernie?"

I insisted, putting out a fist, then removing it and putting out the other. "Elmo?" I said. "Or Ernie?"

Abruptly she understood. "Ernie," she announced.

"Okay," I said. "Good girl. You get Ernie," and I handed her the Ernie toothbrush with a flourish.

"Duh-DA," she told me with a big smile.

"Yes," I said. "Duh-DA." She has learned this from a video.

At a certain point she understood sequencing, first doing one thing and then another, because I had linked it to holding up fingers in order. Next would be "if/ then" clauses, though I had yet to figure out a hand signal for that.

"Let's see . . ." she would say, entering a room and looking around to determine what to do next. I knew she has gotten this phrase, and this intonation, from a video tape of children's songs, but I found it devastating all the same. I loved her ineffectual and mangled attempts to tell knock-knock jokes. I loved the mischievous look she got when she was about to do something she knew I would disapprove of. I loved the fact that if I insisted on something she would, albeit grudgingly, end up doing it.

Our days together were predictable. After a year of intensive therapy she was further along than a year before, though her progress seemed agonizingly slow. I would pick her up on Sunday morning, meeting Martha halfway, at the Naval Academy. Once together, we usually went to a playground, or if the weather was bad, to the mall. She liked going home as well as anything, however, and loved playing with her toys and watching videos, from which she repeated whole sections. In the afternoon, we read, or played, or watched music videos. Then dinner and our evening ritual: take a bath, brush teeth (she resisted, I insisted; it was as regular as clockwork). She got on her pajamas and she hopped into bed to the strains of her "night-night music," a wind-up music box my mother got Martha as a baby shower gift and that had ended up at my house.

Sometimes we looked at a picture book: Alexandra was very good at naming, but she did not follow the logical sequence of a story. Reading a book, therefore, consisted largely of my thinking up things to say about the pictures: "The dog is in front of the car. Say."

"Dog in front of car," she would usually say without further prompting. Did she understand?

"THE dog IS in front of THE car," I would correct her.

"THE dog IS in front of THE car," she would mimic.

I constantly looked for circumstances to teach her the things normal children pick up by themselves: sometimes she was more receptive than others, and I felt I had to take advantage of those moments. We had moved to having therapy in bits and pieces, all day long.

Teaching her "you" and "me," with her propensity to mirror speech, continued to be difficult. "Daddy will pick you up; I will pick you up," I told her when I kissed her goodbye at school.

"Daddy will pick you up," she repeated.

"Daddy will pick ME up," I insisted, hoping that the confusion between my playing her part and speaking for myself would not obscure the point I was trying to make.

"Daddy will pick ME up," she agreed.

Shortly before, she had learned to say, over-emphasizing the possessive, "MY blankie, MY breakfast." Proud of herself, she looked to me for approval, which I gave her instantly.

Sometimes, however, she forgot. "Take your toothbrush," she observed as she picked up her Ernie brush.

"*Whose* toothbrush?" I asked.

She considered. "*My* toothbrush," she announced triumphantly. I kissed the warm top of her hair.

Moments like this made life worth living. Still, the constant strain to be "on" all the time with her took its toll. Once she was in bed, I too was usually so tired that I fell into bed myself. I had to come to terms with the fact that though I have a child, which I had always wanted, this particular child may not be the one I imagined. When I made my wish for offspring, I forgot to put and in, "and may the child not be learning-disabled." There is so much, I sometimes think when I am feeling sorry for myself, that I could teach a more articulate child, a child, in short, more like me. Instead, I think when I become maudlin, I am stuck back at the level of "dog in box."

Winter sun

Most difficult of all was going over the past, like coming to terms with the severing of a limb. By "coming to terms with" we mean that nothing we think about can make things as they were before. But you have to think about it, over and over, until mere repetition convinces us that no, things are not going to go back to being the way they were before. How odd this business of life is, each of us left alone to lick his or her wounds—an exercise pointless in itself, except that it helps the wound to heal and bring nearer the day when we once again can concentrate on other things.

I remember a February Sunday during that time, on a day when Alexandra was back at her mother's, a Sunday saved in memory from the sea of oblivion, when the sun turned the fans of curving verticals of the leafless weeping willow to shining threads draping across and closing the end of the yard. The light, simultaneously diffused and strengthened by its reflection off the snow of the day before, cast the shadow on the wall of a puppet set in a bottle. The mouth of the puppet in a bottle on the sideboard opened sideways in dark elongation against the soft brilliance of the light.

Lying on the sofa and watching the block of light creep across the carpet and outline the leaves of a plant, I opened a volume of Euripides, in English translation, that I had brought home to prepare for teaching Racine's *Phaedra,* based loosely on the Greek tragedy *Hippolytus*. At first, I remember, I was unable to wring sense from the words on the page, being conscious only of the thick paper of the book's pages. I was further distracted by idle memories of the high-ceilinged classrooms where I took Greek philosophy as an undergraduate signed up for courses at Bryn Mawr: the translator, Richard Lattimore, taught in these same musty rooms.

Then an invisible trap door opened, and I was caught in the world of the tragedy. When I looked up again, it was to reflect that Hippolytus, with his spurning of the goddess Artemis, is like my students. His virtues, those of outdoor life linked with his preference for keeping company with other men, are the military virtues, those taught at the Naval Academy.

There was something about this tragedy that fit the lock of my mood this meandering Sunday afternoon during Alexandra's early years, when I was just getting adjusted to the facts of our life together, and the fact that she was all I had to love. Not so much the rather priggish Hippolytus, whose sin was to wish to pass through life unsullied, and so did not do honor to the goddess of love (and is punished for it: this is the primary difference between Euripides' telling of the legend and that of Racine, who is far more interested by Phaedra's boundless feeling of quite Christian sin at her desires). Or perhaps so: the realization that I too wished to pass through life unsullied. Not chaste in the sense of ignorance of sexuality (that he is ignorant of sex is Hippolytus' boast), but instead of having the perfect marriage, of solving all the problems of my new family head-on.

Anything, by contrast, is possible in Euripides' world, I thought: children can die before their times, young wives be led down to the underworld by Death, who is merely claiming a debt. Hippolytus couldn't be saved by the chaste goddess Artemis, she explains, because one god never directly blocks another. Indirectly seems to be fine, and Artemis says she'll just wait until Aphrodite falls in love with a mortal and cause that person harm. The Greeks realized what our whole contemporary world conspires to keep from us, I thought: that we can come to ill through as a result of something other than our own actions, so strangely and without visible pattern that our fates can only be explained as family curses working themselves out, or as the whim of a god or goddess. They realized too that we can be in fact to blame for what happens, though it seems to us that we are without fault.

Only the Greeks, I thought (as Matthew Arnold noted too, listening to the ebb and flow of the waters up Dover Beach) understood the strangely impersonal nature of human suffering; the way a mere change of perspective alters joy to wretchedness, and time or the removal or a generation or two flattens them both so that they can hardly be perceived at all. The way our passions pass over us and through us, like the curl of a wave through water, and leave us powerless. Only the Greeks understood how we can be guilty without having done anything, how our individual actions are useless, though we are condemned to enacting them.

And at this thought of the uselessness but inevitability of individual action, I roused myself from the couch and went in search of a cup of tea, noting that the light had become paler and that the sun would soon have dipped behind the trees. Outside the weeping willow twigs had lost their silvering; night was falling.

Dreams

Some parents dream of having children who will reproduce them. I don't have this dream. Physically beautiful and sunny though Alexandra was even as a tiny child, she had been denied any shred of my particular gift of articulation and ease with language. She is my child, but the world will have many other people in it who, in this sense, will be infinitely more like me than she is. A recent round of tests has confirmed the findings of the earlier ones, that her problems will have to be surmounted step by painful step, bringing her up to the level that normal children attain just by having come unbroken from the womb.

Interacting with Alexandra, I mused as she grew older, was like trying to sing on key with a tone-deaf person. Again and again she misreads body language, misuses expressions: but at least I know it's coming. I explain every non-literal turn of phrase, introduce every concept, warn her of impending changes (a change of routine throws children like her for a loop). She has to be taught to think of others, constantly reminded that someone has gone to trouble to get her a birthday present she merely pushes aside, told that she can't say "I already have that" even if she does—the literalism of autistic children is heart-breaking. They not only never lie, but also don't "get" exaggeration or irony until it's explained: then they get the fact that it's an exception to the rule, but don't understand why until you explain.

Had I only known it, these womb-like early years, just me and her, lying on our stomachs on the floor in a patch of sun, working with the little plastic animals ("Cow *in front of* sheep! Say!") would turn out to be the easiest ones. It was just us, and I loved her. A large portion of the incapability of even slightly autistic people involves social relations with others, people who don't make the endless allowances of people who love us.

Elementary school went relatively well, because it's a small school and the kids had always known her. Attempts to have other girls over were of course disastrous: all she wanted to do was watch TV, and the other little girl was inevitably "busy" the next time. And in sixth grade, in the large suburban middle school, where Alexandra followed a special program in a sea of rapidly too-maturing mall-rat girls, things fell apart: her legs were shredded with her fingernails digging into them; she was frustrated, unhappy, and tense. Things got better when we put her in the first special school, and even better in the second.

It's unclear what adulthood will hold for Alexandra, but in any case having her as my daughter has completely cured me of the disease of most parents of seeing the present as mere prelude to the future: Where will they go to college? Whom will they marry? What profession will they enter? With Alexandra we'll be doing well if she's happy. As for the rest, we'll figure it out—or not. Who knows? She speaks blithely of marriage and children, but relationships with others necessary to sustaining a marriage are almost always beyond autistic adults. To outsiders, they always come off as selfish and uncaring. I know she isn't selfish: she just doesn't know how to think about others unless the adults around her explain it to her. All of her reactions to the world are learned reactions, many of them learned from me. I spend my time trying to help bring her up to normal, able to survive when her mother and I are gone. That's all parents do anyway.

Left behind

I've accepted: what choice do I have? Things are as they are; this isn't about me, after all. Still, when Alexandra was a tiny girl and we two sat for meals around my tiny kitchen table, there were times when the gulf between the way I thought things were going to be and the way they have turned out yawned so large it threatened to swallow me whole.

One day when, trying to phone Martha to discuss some logistical matter regarding Alexandra, I got Jane on the phone instead. Her voice was pleasant, neutral. I heard the guarded tones, the defensive crouch of a seventeen-year-old who is determined to remain polite but not allow herself to be reached. When she called me anything it was "Bruce" rather than "Dad," but if I join end to end the minutes of contact I have had with her since leaving the house, they could be contained in the time of a single one of Alexandra's tooth-brushings.

At first I tried to keep up the relationship with Jane and Sally, grimly telling myself that whatever the adults were up to, it couldn't be allowed to affect the children. Or at least, not Jane, who of the two was clearly guiltless, a supernumerary in a drama fought out between her mother, her stepfather, and her sister. This was a sunny child, a sensitive child, a caring child, an intelligent child, the child who learned everything, the perfect one. This is the child I saw turn into an adolescent; this is the child whose confused attempts to bond with males included plastering herself against me at age 11 or 12 to the point where I had to explain to her gently that though I loved hugging her, this was a bit too much. This was the child who always thought of the other person, who accepted what she was told: in some ways, perhaps, too much the model child. I almost came to see how her mother could have turned her into a little adult at the age of eight, making of her a child-confidante.

Then all that was left was the cool voice on the phone, the pointed absence of any form of address. "I'll get mom," she said.

After the separation, I invited Jane to things: dance performances I was going to, a lunch date. She turned me down every time, always with a plausible excuse, always smilingly. Even I cannot take continual rejection, and I stopped.

I don't think Martha consciously turned Jane against me. I think it more likely that after losing two fathers, Jane decided enough was enough, and withdrew from me. She, like Martha, deals with things by not dealing with them. I imagine this will come back to haunt her later in life.

Sometimes I wanted to cry the deep cry of utter loss that I sometimes, in my most self-pitying moments, thought my situation merited. A friend in England with whom I had had no contact with for a number of years called. I had to bring her up to date on all the changes that had occurred. "I thought you had it all," she observed, somewhat insensitively.

Theresa's call evoked visions of the way it all must have looked from the outside, at about the time of my wedding, or a little after, like a dream come true: childhood sweethearts, a family knit together, the two small blonde children calling me "Daddy" and Martha and me so much in love. Indeed it looked this way to me, who was presumably on the inside. Yet as it turned out, this so-perfect-seeming scenario held within itself the seeds of its own destruction, which were simply unseen both from the outside and by the people involved in it. What point is there in postulating a situation that really never was, which is to say this perfect situation without the blight that ultimately rotted it from within, and feeling sorry for myself because things didn't turn out that way? I had only to lean down to kiss the top of Alexandra's silken hair as she sat in my lap, reading a book, see her running toward me with her arms outstretched and a smile on her face, yelling "Daddy!" to wonder what I had done to deserve this bliss.

Is there a bottom line to life? No, given that our attitude depends on the story we tell ourselves. My mother could be in mourning for her own hellish marriage that consumed the better part of her life, or for her dead son. Instead she arrived smiling twice a week to be Grandma to my daughter, delighted in Alexandra's progress, baked cookies with her, and comforted her when she cries. Happiness depends on the comparisons we choose for ourselves, the framing we put around our own situation: compared with an ideal world, all of us are bad off. Compared with a worse one, all of us are in good shape. And who is to say which is the proper comparison? If we lose something, we never really had it: things are as they are, no more and no less.

Seven
BEGINNING AGAIN

What then?

My friend Laura, confidante and colleague, talked me into advertising for women in the personals of what at that point was, she said, the best "meat market" in town, the *Washingtonian* magazine. Laura had left her husband of nineteen years several years before out of what for him was a clear blue sky, and spent some time making up for the dating years she had never had by playing the field. She swore by the *Washingtonian* personals, and even offered to write mine. My first impulse was to brush aside her suggestion. Jane Austen would never have approved, nor probably Miss Manners, my spiritual mother—or so I argued. You're supposed to get to know people gradually, I protested, while going about living. Personals stripped away all the delicious pretense that forms the fabric of the social world. Laura smiled and said she understood, but that I had to do it anyway. She also suggested we should reflect on the preponderance of bad marriages in Jane Austen, and the fact that the women in her world are condemned to wait with folded hands to see what fate may bring their way during the few brief years that biology and social mores allotted them to finding a husband. Placing an ad to find a partner admits that we are forever past that world where people knew people. But who says that's a bad thing?

I become convinced that Laura was right by reflecting on the columns of matrimonial ads that fill every major Indian newspaper, where I lectured and visited several times during this period. I was fascinated by how utterly stripped of cant and pretense they were. They were brief and to the point, and did not beat around the bush about what they are looking for. These Indian adverts specified caste and sub-caste; skin tone, that great Indian obsession ("wheatish" is the top of the heap); education (USA or Britain are best for men; "convent-educated," which apparently means simply fluent in English, for women), and financial requirements or prospects for women and men, respectively. To be sure, these are matrimonial ads, and I was interested in "meetamonials," as Indian friends called them in our discussions on the topic, but the idea was the same. Why not specify what it is that you want? Maybe that way you'll actually get it.

I began by answering a few ads placed by women and looked forward to the end of the month when a new issue would be in racks in the grocery checkout line. Every month there was a handful that looked possible. (Nowadays that this is instant, on the Internet, such lags of time seem inconceivable.) I answered, either by letter or phone, the ads that interested me, through a box number at the magazine. The placer of the ad retrieved the responses, went through them, and communicated with those she wanted to. There usually followed a chat on the phone to see if I was a jerk. Then, usually, we'd meet for lunch: women were cautioned to be sure to rendezvous in a public place, and let someone know where they were going. In addition, not having totally given up my notion that there's supposed to be some connection with the person you go out with, I joined a listing service whose hook is that it is open only to graduates of "elite" colleges—a poor substitute for the world of everyone knowing everyone of Austen, but perhaps as good as we could do in the late twentieth century. Still I thought: there were a lot of women in college whom I never would have gone out with. Why, merely because it is twenty years later, was having been at such a college a good reason for going out with them? Perhaps simply because I was no longer in college?

I wrote the same letter over and over and sent them off with a photo of myself and my daughter I had had copied 100 times—I figured that was a nice round number: 100 tries ought to produce one result. It felt like putting messages into bottles and throwing them into the ocean. I had no idea if anyone would ever write back; I was putting on a show for someone who might throw me in the trash can. I performed, and others looked or did not, as they chose. Still, being used to sending out such messages in bottles–every blind submission of writing is like this—I tried to write the same thing over and over with a modicum of good humor, and without worrying too much about details: there's no way to know what the person will take to, so you might just as well do what you want and hope for the best. Besides, I didn't really know if I wanted to know the person I was writing to, though of course the game required me to act as if I did.

A few days after trying my first round of both magazine and college ads, there was a message on my machine, the first of many: "Hi. I'm Barbara (or Sarah, or Jane). I'm responding to your letter"—or, if it was an ad from the *Washingtonian,* to which I soon added the Washington tabloid *City Paper*, "your message"—in some cases one left recorded messages at a central telephone number.

But Barbara wasn't the one. Neither was Sarah or Jane, a succession of other too-old-for-me workaholics who dressed badly and talked too rapidly, all deafeningly sharing the sound of their biological clock. Whatever made me me took second (or third, or fourth) place to the things I couldn't help, that made me generically a Good Biological Match. Yet somehow I had to get through the evening. Typically my date and I would go out to dinner at a restaurant in Washington. I paid, knowing in most cases that I would never see the woman again, thanked her for the evening, and shook hands. I learned not to promise to call.

Reactions from the woman's side varied: usually she was interested in me, sometimes she wasn't. One twenty-something woman whom I found pretentious but very good-looking had a very negative reaction indeed: we saw one another through the window of the restaurant and I saw her step slow, then lurch forward again as she saw me looking at her. We got through dinner somehow until I asked her, as I felt I had to just for the record, whether she would be interested in pursuing things. Though flustered, she managed to say that she would not be, whereupon I thanked her for the evening, left money for the check, and hit the road for home. Clearly she was looking for something else than I could provide: there was no point in trying to figure out what. There are only a few matches for us in a world of misses; most of us aren't so aware of this as I became because they're not looking.

I had two dates with a woman who turned out, small world, to be one of the psychiatrists who was peripherally involved in Sally's treatment. She was a bony hyper woman with tight black hair, who was very aware of her slightly brown skin inherited from her Egyptian father. Still, she was attractive. Following up her signals, I suggested on the second date (which was dinner at my house), that I would like to make love to her. Her counter-proposal was that we sleep together with no sex. In my 40s, that seemed ridiculous to me, and in any case something I didn't want to do. If I'd been 20 I might have done something I didn't want to do. But I wasn't. "I'm sorry," I said. "I wouldn't feel comfortable with that. But you've drunk a lot, and I wouldn't want you to have an accident. There are several guest beds. Feel free to choose one."

She did. The next morning I heard the sound of the door closing at an ungodly hour and came downstairs sometime later to find six pages of finely-written cerebrations in a pile on the sofa, going into exhaustive detail about how she had never felt so rejected in her life. I shrugged and threw them away. How could she possibly have thought I'd be interested in her unloading her life on me? It later turned out she had forgotten her coat in her haste to get out of my house, so I had to send it to her. And that was that.

Funkier dates came in response to the ads I placed in the *City Paper*—by now I was getting bolder, putting in ads as well as responding to them. One woman sounded very nice on the phone, said she managed real estate, and sent a picture of herself to alert me that she was black, if that made any difference. I should have been wise to the fact that she was desperate by the fact that after the initial chat setting up our date, she started calling me every day, just to tell me her problems. And then came the face-to-face: the woman who showed up was easily 50 pounds heavier than the woman in the photo. Give her credit for trying, I thought, more bemused than angry. Then there was the extremely tall, very thin artist with the leotards, the spiked hair, and the tennis shoes, whom I met up with in the orchid garden of the Victorian National Arts and Industries Museum in Washington. We went for a sandwich and parted ways. Her current artistic theme was bronze sculptures of leaping animals for parks. She had just gotten a commission for a leaping frog.

Another ad yielded a six-month relationship with a woman whose company and bed I enjoyed but who, I finally realized when I analyzed it, annoyed me with her left-over-student lifestyle, which somehow seemed to me a denial of adulthood. Her husband of twelve years, a man she clearly simultaneously hated and still loved, had left her for another woman. She wanted our relationship to work, she said; to me it felt like treading water. The moment of truth for me was opening her china cabinet and finding a total of three mismatched plates. If she hadn't entered adulthood by now and given up this marginal student lifestyle, it didn't seem likely she was ever going to. Like so many of the women I went out with, she just wasn't a match for me, as I probably am not a match for most women. It's nobody's fault, that's just the way things are. I was sorry to have caused her pain, if I did.

In real life, we can meet and size up people under the guise of doing something else: chatting about the weather, waiting at the water cooler, standing in the checkout line. If you walk away, you can do so under the guise of merely having completed the ostensible, rather than the real, action—which was, checking out the other person. Blind dates take place with no cover, under spotlights: the underbrush has been defoliated. There is only one issue on the table: are you attracted to me? A "no" in answer to this question cannot be brushed away or hidden.

From sexual promiscuity, if you can call a couple of new women a month promiscuity (gay men call promiscuity several tricks a night for several nights in a row), I learned many things. I learned that what the body wants to do sexually is not something we can know until we let it roam a while and see where it goes. We discover all sorts of things about a realm we didn't even know existed. Not that we want to do everything: among other things I discovered the limits of what I was willing to do, or wanted to do. One woman told me after the second date she wanted to penetrate me with a strap-on. I had vowed not to reject anything out of hand, and it was only when I put 2 and 2 together about what other things she wanted to do—have me spank her, for beginners, and masturbate together rather than having me fuck her—that I realized we weren't a match. Another woman, more on my wavelength, wanted me to tie her up. Fine, I thought, until she started talking about how she wished my hair was gray and I was 20 years older than she. That was the end of that, despite her great legs and her obvious desire for me.

What if I'd found myself married to one of these women, say without having tried things out sexually with them? What if we'd married so young that even she didn't know that was what she really wanted? I imagine marriages all over the world where people are even unable to articulate what it is they want, only knowing that what they do with their partner isn't hitting anywhere near the center of the target. People's sexual desires live in a realm that has to be developed, like any other. Many moralists who insist that sex for the sake of sex defiles the "sanctity of the person." But the sexually inexperienced don't know what they want, and chances are against it being what an equally inexperienced partner will want. Even the sexually experienced may have neglected whole parts of their own sexual landscape on which light has yet to shine. You can talk about the sanctity of the person all you want, and why only married, loving sex is okay in the eye of God. But if it makes people unhappy, that for me is the end of it. For this reason, I'm a fan of sex for sex's sake: it teaches you who you are. I had the luxury of simply saying "goodbye" when I realized that I had crossed a line to a place I didn't want to go, or when I understood we simply weren't enough of a fit to make things work. Pity those handcuffed by morality or marriage into sticking around.

My bottom line after years of meeting, sizing up and being sized up, bedding, giving and taking pleasure: that interaction with other people means hurting them and/or being hurt. At least that's the case if the stakes for personal esteem are as high as they are in the no-holds-barred world of sexuality, where people have to get naked—literally and metaphorically—with each other. It's what drives people, scared, back into little old man- and ladydom; it's what produces the language of sexual "morality," which usually means predictability and abstinence.

Jain monks wear gauze masks so as not to inhale small creatures and so take life inadvertently, and who sweep the path before them as they walk: probably we should all do this, but we can't. Face it; you're going to kill a few bugs in your time on Earth. Even a well-meaning person, such as I take myself to be, conscious of the potential for hurt to others and passionately interesting in minimizing that hurt, can inflict it. You don't have to be proud of yourself, but there's not a lot you can do about it either. It comes with the territory. Welcome to life.

I don't know what you're thinking

With time, in my several years back on the meat market, I learned not to over-analyze. Which meant, I realized I'd never know what the other person was thinking. The afternoon I spent with a leggy Harvard-educated blonde made this particularly clear. Each of us had a page of each other's data from the college network, had talked (successfully) on the phone, and had agreed to meet for coffee in the lobby, complete with overstuffed chairs and tea tables, of a Washington hotel. Meeting at 4, we were still there at 8, having talked uninterruptedly for four hours. I was hooked. And, I was convinced, so was she. How otherwise to explain the length of our conversation, its intensity, her laughing at my jokes? It turned out we had a lot in common, among them being that she'd grown up in Munich, where I'd studied, a common background in German literature. She smiled, laughed, made her eyes grow wide, leaned into get closer: all the signals were there. She let me hold the cab door for her, and put her hand on my shoulder before giving me a kiss. I could feel the warmth of her hand for days afterwards.

And that was the last I saw her.

I sent her flowers a few days later, because it was Valentine's Day—a mixed bouquet, not roses (that would have been too much too soon), and of course I had called her the next day to say what a lovely time I'd had. She called to thank me for the flowers, and talked enthusiastically about getting together after her business trip. I had begun counting the days on the calendar till her arrival back in town. When I got no message on the day she was due back, I told myself she was tired. When I got no message the following day, I told myself her flight had been changed. But by the time a week had passed I knew she was out of the picture. Though I knew by this point it was futile, I called to leave a bright and cheery message saying I hoped she'd had a good trip, was looking forward to seeing her again. As I had expected, this too failed to elicit a response. And that would have been that, except that months later I happened on her e-mail address and on impulse wrote to her saying, now that it was clearly over without really having started, could she satisfy my curiosity and tell me what happened? A brief response said that she'd decided to go back to Germany for good and didn't want to start any new relationships in the States.

I don't think this was the reason, and in any case it didn't explain what had clearly been a spike of interest that cooled. What I finally realized was that I'd never know what had really happened, and that in any case there wasn't any point in knowing: it was over. Still, I was new enough at this game that I couldn't help raking over the clearly insufficient evidence I had to try and find a plausible explanation. I couldn't have misread the signals that suggested she was initially as taken with me as I with her. Yet there was one snag in the otherwise seamless cloth that had unraveled before my enraptured gaze that afternoon and evening in the hotel while the harpist played and went on break, played again and went away, before finally pulling the cover over her instrument for the evening. And this was the snag that could, I thought, explain her otherwise puzzling behavior. For despite her attractiveness and her apparent response to the male signals I was sending out to her, she had said her last relationship (our conversation covered all bases) had ended three years before, had lurched along for a year, and had come to its end when she realized she wasn't attracted to the man.

No relationships for three years? Of any kind? More to the point, I wondered— wondering at the same time if I was judging this from too male a perspective—How can you be with someone for a year you decide you aren't attracted to? Surely this is something you have to be aware of at the outset of a relationship? And if this man didn't do it for her, surely she had no lack of other candidates. It all seemed odd, suggesting a deep-seated what? Frigidity? Lack of libido? Fear? Not the physical openness I thought I had sensed in her.

I appealed for advice to Laura, who confirmed from my description of our interaction that my date had been attracted to me, and went on to suggest that she had at the same time been fearful, perhaps precisely because of some underlying coldness or "issue" with men. She had dealt with her fear, Laura suggested, by dropping me. My take-home point is: I'll never know; the mere fact that she acted as she did indicates that she wasn't the one for me. In most of life we never know.

Win some, lose some. Probably someone is going to be hurt. You, the other person, perhaps both. But not playing at all isn't an option.

Body and soul

In high school I was contemptuous of people who wanted to be known for their physical selves. In college at Haverford, there weren't people like this; the guys who were athletic tended to be runners, or soccer players whose tongue-in-cheek goal was to "Beat Swat," as we called neighboring rival Swarthmore. When I graduated I was weedy, pasty, and a bit pudgy, despite my height. I moved in with Keith, and went every day to the library to write and read. Things changed on this score, as on so many others, that summer I was nineteen. Along about July, I suddenly noticed that when I climbed the three levels of stairs to "my" room to write for the day, I could hear my breath reverberating in my ears as if a diver's inside of his helmet. For the first time in my life, I remember, I was conscious of my body as something that might be in danger, or that I should think about.

Or was it only that I was then entering adulthood, responsible primarily to myself, defining myself by what I wanted to do and not against some inadmissible outside pressure? Now I see my students constantly defining themselves against outside forces, and want to explain to them that maturity does not come this way. That afternoon, at any rate, I had a revelation. After years of having to prove to others by rejecting sports that I was smart, suddenly I realized that I didn't have to prove anything to anybody; I could do what I wanted to do. The problem was, I hadn't realized until that moment that I wanted to do it.

Gesagt, getan, as the German aphorism so succinctly has it; "no sooner said than done," is English's wordier version. That very evening, in the suddenly less relentless air of evening that follows on the relentless afternoons of Washington summer, I went out to the playing field complex across from where we lived wearing a pair of tattered tennis shoes, resolving to run around the soccer field until I collapsed. On the other side of the playing fields were the gas tanks that rose and fell in their girders depending on depletion level, dwarfing everything around them. I made it precisely two and a half times around the soccer field before a giant hand reached down my throat and ripped my guts out. The nausea of the mile I had to run every spring in junior high school was nothing compared to it.

The next evening I tried again. And the next evening. And the next. I don't remember if it was immediately less painful, or if it took several weeks for me to adjust to this new and horrible, if strangely energizing, sensation. At any rate it was a challenge. Because I was setting this challenge for myself, it had to be met. Similar challenges that others had been setting for me all these years had to be rejected, precisely because they were coming from the outside.

Soon, I was doing ten laps around the soccer field, then five laps around the entire complex, then ten, then twenty, and at some point in the following months was running the ten miles into Washington down to the Capitol and back again. I found that contrary to my deepest-held beliefs, I was strong and athletic, and could push my body to great lengths before it rebelled. And when it did, I could try and push it more. I discovered the feeling of reaching the edge of myself: every day, in writing, every evening, in running, sucking up glorious air, becoming one with the balmy summer, hardly feeling my legs or the ground beneath me.

I also remember elaborate and extremely pleasureful masturbation sessions: masturbation rather than a relationship because I simply didn't have the mental room for another human being. It wasn't a quick jerk into a Kleenex; it involved elaborate stroking and slowing games that could easily last an hour and that, I am convinced, made me a much more involved lover when I once again became active with partners. Knowing from my own body how many games could be played short of orgasm made me eager to try them out on women: one girlfriend told me that making love with me was like entering a Vogue picture: at once completely mannered and completely natural. In this as in other things, I came to others through myself. Most people do it the other way, taking the social for granted and never reaching as far inside them as themselves.

In the difficult years that followed, it was running, I'm sure, that kept me on an even keel. In Chicago, I ran along the Midway. In the dead of winter I would come in with the full beard I wore at the time covered with my own breath turned to ice. In Munich, I ran in the Nymphenburg Gardens nearby the house I lived in, and developed problems with ligament separation from running on the concrete paths alongside the canal. That taught me to be careful about hard surfaces, and to alternate running with swimming.

I started lifting weights in graduate school at Vanderbilt, when I was finally able to bring myself to acknowledge that there was nothing wrong with wanting to be more muscular than my jogging and swimming was making me. Showing that much interest in your body had until then seemed somewhat embarrassing; intelligent people were supposed to be above that. I had a beginner's weight bench that I put away behind the door, to the extent that that was possible, of my tiny student apartment, laboriously taking all the plates off and stacking them in a closet after a work-out. In Freiburg, getting more hard-core, I belonged to a real gym, with Universal machines and free weights, whose owner was a hulk named Bruno who showed me the routine I used faithfully and, perhaps, somewhat blindly, for two years. In Rwanda, I had to make do with a contraption consisting a stiff rubber cable attached to stirrups at both ends and made solid in the middle by a rigid piece of movable plastic with a ridge down the side to accommodate the cable. Using this, I could do a reasonable approximation of a "real" workout—or so it seemed at the time. With a pull-up bar, crunches for the abs, and a daily run down the rutted, unpaved road between the potato fields where the old women bent over the harvest would look up and stare and the children herding sheep along the side of the road would stop and wave at the crazy "muzungu" (white person) with all that energy to waste on running for no apparent purpose, I made do.

The academics whose ranks I later joined tend to downplay the body as I once did. But with them, as with my youthful self, I discovered, it's all sour grapes, their sneaking fascination with physical glamour becoming clear in recent years as academic attention has turned to fashion, dolls, and pop singers. They don't even dress well. What a horror, the annual Modern Language Association conference, where tens of thousands of tweedy mismatched professors who never crack a sweat swamp a major North American city between Christmas and New Year's.

Accepting the mirror
The weight room, where I've gone regularly since arriving in Annapolis, has allowed the inner me to finally merge with the outer. Going to the weight room, for all except those who are doing it in the service of some sport and who are sent there by the coach, means accepting the mirror. We pump iron because of what we want to look like. This means, accepting as a first step that you're not happy with the way you do look: it's not by chance that so many professional body-builders started as 98-lb. weaklings, and gravitate so quickly to quick-result means like steroids. The seeds of looking better than average is the conviction, the realization and the admission, that you look worse than average. Sometimes the tortoise does win the race.

Men aren't complex. All other things being equal, they want to hang out with the guys with the big arms and chest, and fuck the women with the big boobs. Living around the military as I have done for going on two decades, in an institution imbued by the Marine Corps ethos of square jaw and bulging biceps, I've come to understand it's primarily other men who are impressed by gym muscles, and the push- and pull-ups these allow. I know it's not women. And men like to show off to other men: if you've got it, flaunt it. Men who work out—certainly my students—seek every opportunity to strip off their shirts and show off. Hallowe'en at the Naval Academy is an excuse for the men to take off their clothes; the "pep rallies" we used to have were the same, with hundreds of half-naked ripped guys carrying on. They've stopped those as unseemly, and have even forbidden the plebes to get shirtless in that annual rite of passage, the climb up the greased obelisk known a "Herndon." Why else do soccer players rip off their jerseys in moments of joy except to show off their physiques? In that moment, they're allowed to betray the same desire for admiration of our pecs we all feel.

It took me years to admit it: I want other guys to think I look good. Of course, other guys don't actually tell you you look good or that they admire you, at least not directly. The world is a zero-sum game in the guy universe. If you look good, that's a threat to them, so they're likely to pretend they didn't notice, or go back to grunting even harder themselves. Only close friends late at night, probably after a couple of beers, will compliment each other. And it will always be in the form of a half-criticism, half-compliment, always laced with obscenities. "Shit, you're a fuckin' animal!" they might say. Or in the gym, indirectly: "What's your secret for biceps?" they might ask. Of course, you can't let on you know it's a compliment. You have to pretend you understand it as a request for information and treat your biceps as if they're not yours, but someone else's. So you talk a little about your favorite exercise, which he isn't really listening to. He's just bonding. Then you slap the other guy on the shoulder, and tell him he's "getting huge" too.

"See ya, dude," you say to him.

"Yeah, see ya," he says, and goes back to his own exercises, studiedly avoiding looking at you, or your reflection in the mirror.

"Sir, you're ripped!" a student of mine said in a combination of approbation and surprise one day when he saw me doing biceps curls in the gym. He hadn't even imagined I had a body. His reaction was to a degree involuntary; he could get away with expressing it because, being the professor, I wasn't his competition. He would never have done this with a younger man. But if he'd missed that first moment of surprise at seeing me out of a suit, it would have been difficult to come back to it; he'd have had to pretend he took me for granted. Men can't all of a sudden give another man a compliment on the way he looks. It implies they've been thinking about it.

Be a male model! Or just look like one!

All this was, I'm sure, revenge on my past. It turned out I wasn't finished yet. It helped me, in this final phase of losing my physical inhibitions, that my male students are frank in their panting pursuit of "big guns" and spend a lot of time in what seems to me the happy homoeroticism of showing off for each other physically. If they could do this, so could I.

One day as I was lounging on a bench in front of the Hirshhorn Museum in Washington, waving at Alexandra, then six, each time she came around the merry-go-round, a woman who seemed like something out a modern version of the Brothers Grimm—a cigarette crushed between her gnarled fingers, hair a color that did not go with her wrinkled skin—stood abruptly before me. With no introduction, she suddenly began to speak in a raspy voice. "Have you ever thought of modeling? I'm a talent scout for a modeling school."

Who was this creature? Had she been summoned by desires I didn't even know I had? Not, certainly, by the particular desires of that day and place—which were more devoted to hoping Alexandra was having fun and wondering if I would have time to take a nap when we got home—but perhaps by those too deep for articulation. "What about your daughter?" the crone added. "She'd be a natural!" How did she know which child was my daughter, or that any one was? Had she been watching us together? Or did she simply know all about us?

At the time, Alexandra looked, as a friend said, like the pictures of children you get in frames at the store to fill up the space till you put in the less attractive people of your own set, with peach-like-skin, strawberry blonde hair, and blue eyes. Yet even at six the implications of her learning disability were clear: the need for endless repetition, a difficulty in abstracting. Once I thought I'd settle for nothing less in a daughter than a Wellesley graduate. Then I'd been forced to realize that cheerleader or yes, model, might not be so bad. Somebody has to check out this modeling business, I had begun to think, for Alexandra if not for me. But yes, for me too. With its echoes of the sad advertisements in the backs of a hundred magazines, the idea was intrinsically appealing in a kind of masochistic way. "Be a Model! Or Just Look Like One!" "Modeling! It's a Man's Job!" Try typing in "Models" on the Internet to be convinced that most of the world wants this kind of attention: all the sites open with some variation of "So you want to be a model!" A school, furthermore, was an emotional safety net. If I didn't succeed, I could tell myself I wasn't really interested. And this school, the temptress went on to explain, was connected with an apparently reputable agency that guaranteed representation for the graduates of the program. From what I had understood, getting an agency to take you was the biggest hurdle.

At the same time, I was savvy enough to be suspicious that this was nothing but a scam. And so it largely turned out to be. The school, deemed to be engaged in misleading business practices such as these very "talent scouts" to prey on the vanity of people like myself with a craving for public valorization, was slapped with a federal suit and closed, but not before it had declared bankruptcy and defaulted on many of its bills. What it taught was allowed to be legitimate enough; the issue was whether it had misled the gullible into thinking they would be on the cover of *Vogue* as a result. I had no such illusions, and it served its purpose for me.

The initial interview was initially for Alexandra. At that point, the company was still riding high, operating from flashy digs in a building near the upscale Tyson's Corner Mall in Northern Virginia, outfitted with lots of lights and marble, and staffed with beautiful blonde and black receptionists that looked as if they had in fact stepped out of *Vogue*.

The young "VP for Talent" (VP seemed about as low down as people with offices went)—also blonde, also gorgeous—tried to explain things to her, to whom I had purposely explained very little.

"Do you watch movies with real children?" she asked. Alexandra allowed as she did. "Those children are models," said the VP. Alexandra regarded her with horror.

I made a quick decision. TV and videos were one of the few things Alexandra really seemed to like. She believed in them faithfully. "I've changed my mind," I said. Time enough later, I thought, for her to be told not only that Barney was an annoying man in a dinosaur suit, but that those even more annoying children that seemed so happy all the time were being paid to be so.

Then, my heart thumping, I decided I had to take a chance. "What about me?" I asked abruptly.

Should I despise myself for asking? Was I pitiful? I'd say I was trying to convince myself my youth wasn't gone, but at 20 I wouldn't have been able to bring myself to ask it. At least now I could admit I wanted to know

The gorgeous VP sat back and considered. Was I about to be handed my come-uppance?

"I could see that," she finally said. I exhaled. Then: "Could you show me your teeth?"

There followed a "screen test" for a video camera, and a waiting period of three days at the end of which I was to come in to learn my fate. So far as I know, all comers were accepted. Yet, as my particular gorgeous VP reasonably pointed out, the agency had to be willing to represent you once you finished. Was it only as a stage prop that she had prominently displayed on her desk a pile of papers whose top application was stamped "Rejected" in red ink? I decided to do it. The lessons weren't cheap, but I told myself it was money I could afford to lose. I knew I'd never have the nerve to try to become a model on my own.

In the ensuing months I learned many things. I was fussed over for photo shoots, videotaped by the acting teacher, told what "products" to wash my face with (I'd never heard of toner), and put through my paces by a leggy ex-model with a mop of hair, and fabulous attitude. She went under the single name of Demetria, and also did makeup. In the parlance, this made her a "makeup artist." The aspiring actors and models with me were called "the talent," as in the photographer's harried question: "Has the talent arrived?"

Wanting it

The first day of class, Demetria went around the room and asked, "Why are you here?" She started with me. Trying to protect myself, I went for the self-deprecating and said, "For fun." The others, equally scared, picked up my cue and echoed me.

Demetria was highly displeased, and began flinging her arms around. "You aren't here for FUN! You have to be here because this MATTERS to you! You gotta want it! Say after me, I want it!"

"I want it," we echoed half-heartedly.

"LOUDER!" she insisted.

"I WANT IT!" we screamed.

"All right," she said, appeased, and leaned back in her chair.

She was right. At some level, we did want it.

The fashion model's biggest asset is his or her walk. This walk is a learned skill; the men project "male" to the viewer, as the women telegraph "female." One of my fellow students was a gorgeous, pouty Oriental girl who barely spoke English but who jutted her hips out as if to the manner born. The key to the female runway walk, it turned out, was a pelvic bone jut and an exaggerated cantalievering motion. "Hips!" Demetria would scream, and the aspiring models would accentuate the tilting up and down to the point where I simply waited for Demetria to shake her head in despair. To my great surprise, she was delighted. In this business, more clearly was more.

If girls were all about hips, guys were all about shoulders. The male walk overlaps with normal motion in that it emphasizes perfect uprightness, achieved (so it seemed to me) by tilting slightly backwards at the hips and resisting the impulse to drop the chest to compensate. The sensation I had was that of presenting my pecs on a platter to the sky. Then you drop the face, but without making a double chin. All of this causes a swing in the shoulder yoke, and makes the arms follow along, rather than being the initiators of the swing. It also lengthens the stride, as the legs move more as whole units rather than as bendables. The result is the rolling gait of a John Wayne, with the arms held out slightly from the sides, as if ready to grasp a gun in a holster, or the side-to-side slouch of a young athlete whose wing-like lats push his arms out from his sides.

The major flaw of my walk, it turned out, was holding my chin too high. "Chin DOWN!" Demetria would scream at me as we took turns walking down the "runway" in front of mirrors. Even I could see that I was stiff. Imagine all those people looking at me!

If we guys majored in shoulders, we minored in glowering. Fashion models, male and female, do not smile. The exception seemed to be what Demetria referred to as her "plus models," the well-endowed girls with big behinds, who were told to smile as if there was no tomorrow. We men learned to assume a wide-legged more-guy-than-guy stance at the end of the runway. All of us learned how to take off a coat (let it slide off your shoulders, catch it before it falls). We learned how to turn. "Practice your walks!" Demetria would exhort us at the end of every lesson.

Demetria herself had had a brief career as a model in Milan. "What happened?" we asked, when after several lessons we had bonded with her. "They couldn't decide whether I was white or black," she told us airily. "Over there that gives them problems."

Not all the women were gorgeous as the Asian girl, nor all the men striking. A couple of the women were mousy; I wondered how they ever hoped to pull off this act. Yet I envied one young man in the class for his Arrow-shirt-man good looks and his utter unself-consciousness. He was very gifted at running his hands through his hair, "looking" at the imaginary audience, and slinging a coat over his shoulder. How could he have gotten over my besetting fear, that of looking ridiculous? Thinking of Kleist's image of the marionettes that danced the most perfect dance because they could not think, I pegged him as a vapid beauty, as well as my most threatening competition, precisely because he was unaware of the intrinsically ridiculous aspect of everything we were doing. But of course this sense of superiority on my part was self-destructive. I could insist on my knowledge, and let it defeat me, or I could go beyond it, and get where others, less self-conscious, had started out. Becoming nothing but a body: it was a challenge. Keep trying, I told myself: chin up—or rather, chin down.

Acting class was equally challenging. For my first role, I was given a phrase that, I was told, came from TV spots for a chain restaurant, just six words. "For the seafood lover in you."

No aspiring Hamlet ever pored longer over his part than I over the subtleties of this phrase. For the SEAFOOD lover in you (swallowing the final prepositional phrase)? For the seafood lover in YOU? It held many mysteries. I was horrified when I saw the tapes of this: could I really be opening my eyes that wide? Bill, our affable bear of a teacher (who had actually had a real role, albeit a non-speaking one, on the TV show "Homicide"), told me I had to rein it in. "The camera sees everything," he said. "You're using stage eyes." Or a professor's, I thought to myself.

Then on to commercial print, which, it turned out, was all about teeth. The teacher, a local photographer, insisted that whatever you were selling, you had to look as if you were having the time of your life doing it. He leafed through several magazines, stopping at the ads, to prove his point. Whatever the product, from wine (the pretty couple clinking glasses in a restaurant) to a product for seniors, which showed a gray-haired couple frolicking in a field, teeth ruled. "You have to smile yourself silly," he insisted.

Silly is just what it seemed to me. This too caused problems. Some of my problems were undoubtedly those of the professor used to being listened to, controlling the situation. Some of them were probably just because I'm a man. Because being looked at for our physical selves is the ultimate worship of being, as opposed to doing, it's the pole traditionally assigned to the female in our society: this is precisely the hurdle I had to get over. "Male model" is still a somewhat suspect term, and of course the necessity for the adjective shows just how odd the whole concept is: models are female unless declared otherwise.

The camera is flat

Demetria was right: you have to want it, not to mention spend the money trying to get it. Even those who bypass the model schools (which are out to make money, and are selling the dream of making the big time) and go directly to an agency have to pay for their own promotional materials, as I did: the photos for the "comp card," another chunk of hundreds of dollars. From these photos I learned several things: one is that the camera sees things flat. You can stick out your chin towards the camera to sharpen the silhouette; the result will just be good, not goofy as it seems to you: you're out to have an effect.

I went to the house of the photographer, Mark, and his stylist wife Paulette. Paulette chose a box-cut bathing suit from the handful I had bought ("makes your long torso look shorter") and Mark strung up a black background in front of his garage door. "The light is right," he said. "It'll emphasize your abs." I had been worried about a pimple on my neck, but it disappeared in a swipe of makeup. Paulette sprayed me with oil, then with water, so the droplets stood on my shining skin. "It's cold," said Mark. "That's good. It'll make your nipples hard." I was supposed to be fooling with a pair of goggles around my neck. "Don't raise your arms so high," Mark told me. "It's flattening out your pecs." When he told me he was going to shoot I tensed my pecs and arms and sucked in my gut in what Arnold calls a "vacuum." It hurts.

So there's nothing natural about what the model in a photograph is doing. The most interesting fact for me in all this was learning that even with all this artifice, it's rare when as many as half the pictures in a shoot are usable, and one or two are always the best. And it's the best one the audience always sees. When the proofs came back we had lengthy discussions about which ones to use on the cards. Finally I received two small packages of the finished product. I mailed the packages out to the half a dozen agencies in the area. Then I waited again.

Getting signed is all a matter of having the right "look." One agency liked my "look" but said I was too similar to a model they already represented. One agency, that also admired my "look," added me to their list of hand models. (Talk about fetishization of the body!) The director of another agency insisted that in a few years I'd be working as much as their top model, whose card she showed me, a gray-haired, mid-height, not particularly striking man. I didn't know whether to take this as a compliment or not.

It turned out that my work on my walk was probably in vain: all were agreed that I was too old for fashion, which in any case is not big in the Washington area. Not to mention that I was too healthy looking. "Look at *GQ*!" one agent insisted. "They're all underfed!" Despite this, my so-artificial comp card joined the dozens of other cards arranged alphabetically on my agents' walls, with all the hopeful Bills and Johns and Martins, as well as Beckys, Tammys, and Sallys.

Soon the phone began to ring, albeit very intermittently. (Advice for aspiring models: don't quit your day job—but if you have a day job, how can you take modeling jobs on a day's notice?) I was called to be in a workout video, one of the muscle boys in the background who flexes while the star explains things in front (all my hours in the weight room paying off). I was an extra in a movie, one of whose scenes was being shot on the street in front of the Watergate in Washington. My job, after waiting around in the extras' "holding room" for four hours, was to cross the street on Virginia Avenue wearing a blue suit and carrying a raincoat (along with twenty-five other people doing roughly the same thing and dressed in roughly the same manner) until the director said "Re-set," then do it again. The waiting room was full of union-member actors hired to sit in gridlocked cars outside the hotel, or to cross the street like me. In another shoot I was asked to put on a blue spandex bodysuit and be an oxygen molecule, grouped with two female hydrogen molecules, also in their spandex suits. In another, I was a weary businessman sending out mailings the old-fashioned way rather than the new-tech way, and was posed before a pile of envelopes to be sealed with a sponge in my mouth and my glasses askew. In another, I lounged around high-end apartments that were converting to condos and needed "residents" to be standing in the kitchens with a glass of wine, doing a pump in the workout room, or chatting with the concierge, all for the advertising booklet they were producing.

These were the high-end jobs, where I knew in advance that the client wanted me, and would pay me to photograph me. Sometimes it was only a "go-se," the model's equivalent of an audition with a hundred or two hundred other people. One hot afternoon I braved the Baltimore Beltway to get to a studio where dozens of mommies clutching headshots of their children were milling about. The client, a car brand, wanted to take audition tapes of dozens of people, men, women and children, to put together a single prototypical family. I answered a few questions for the camera and left. I never even got a rejection, though I wasted the afternoon: "Modeling! It's a buyer's market!"—that's what the ads in the magazines should say. Was I too tall? Too dark-haired? Too smiley? Not smiley enough? Had they already chosen by the time they got to me on the tape? Did they ever get to me? Sever months later I became briefly sort-of famous: my hugely enlarged face was plastered across a chain of East Coast banks in posters that asked, "Is there business checking that comes with extras I really want?" I came in three sizes as part of this campaign, small, medium, and the window-size. I was up for months.

Periodically I get a check for a few hundred dollars. It's not enough to pay the mortgage—or even, yet, cover the cost of the school. What I get out of it is valorization: Yes, the camera tells me, you really are a good-looking dude. Does it show a weakness of character that I accept this adulation rather than rejecting it with a snort?

Eight
HAPPY FAMILIES

Until the day I left Martha I would have said I was happy; it was only the great sense of relief afterwards that convinced me I hadn't been. During the period of bachelordom that followed, I would have said I was happy. Yet if the point of all that dating was to end this period, perhaps I wasn't. If you have to ask if you're happy, you probably aren't. And if you don't ask, it doesn't matter.

All those blind dates finally, in what seemed like the Nth hour, bore fruit: just when I was about to despair, my eyes blurring at all the blind dates, the one night stands, and the one-month-affairs, I met Meg, now my wife. She was one of ten or a dozen new college listings that particular month, to whom I dutifully wrote the same letter I had already written dozens of times before, enclosing the same photograph of myself with Alexandra (of the original 100 photos perhaps ten remain). One day more than a month later Meg called me to follow up, though her name by that point meant nothing to me as I hadn't paid much attention to it initially and in any case had moved on. She had, it turned out, initially set aside my letter, putting it into the "reject" pile: she didn't want to marry someone with children. I was, after all, damaged goods. Still, after a couple of non-starters for her, she had come back to my letter, apparently thinking, Why not?

Now she tells me it was meant to be. I love her, and love my life, but I don't know how we can say such a thing was meant to be. I, after all, thought the same thing with Martha. And what if Meg hadn't called me back? The "meant to be"s are all chosen from the things that were, just as the 50 Most Beautiful People in the World are chosen by *People* magazine from the people well-known enough to be on the list from which these are chosen.

Our first little boy was born in 2002, our second in 2004. Alexandra then still lived half the week with me. They have become my life; it seems that Meg has always been my wife. I take my new life so for granted that on those rare occasions when for whatever reason I get a flash of my prior life—something Alexandra says or does reminds me of her half-sisters at her age, people who have for me ceased to be—I rear back in puzzlement, furrowing my brow at the world it calls up that I had thought utterly dead, and that apparently is only slumbering inside me. I catch a shredded wisp of a vanished smell, and feel like Proust trying to remember what it was. Like Proust, I try, and back off, try again. And then I usually get it: a scene in the present fits perfectly with the fragment in the past. It evokes in its entirety, like the madeleine and the taste of the herbal tea that calls back Combray, a scene in my now-vanished life, with two small blonde daughters and a wife I had been friends with since childhood, with the sense, intermittent even at the time, of having achieved a perfect marriage with my own past, having closed the circle, made up the lack of father to two little girls, and the lack of husband to my wife, having brought the world into consonance. Or it brings back with jarring intensity of the sense of being dragged off at 90 miles an hour by a force I knew I should resist, that I had to resist if I was to be a responsible human being and a man, but that everyone in my world was pleading with me to give in to.

Such visitations from the past makes it clear to me that I can still enter these self-enclosed worlds, but there's no purpose. They're like tape loops, endlessly cycling in on themselves. They never change, they're never added to. I learn nothing from them; they are my own personal hells, doomed in Dantesque fashion to repeat endlessly the same mistakes, hear the same things, respond in the same way. What I couldn't have predicted was the fact that, once put back in the bottle by the mere passage of time and the stopper firmly on again, such genii become inaudible, their shrieks and cries held within the container from which they had been loosed, and then simply shrunk to the point were, with a gulp, I could merely swallow it like a pill. Perhaps in its own world it has importance, something suggested by the unsettling ferocity with which it can return if I am ever unwise enough to pull the stopper off again. Only I know enough not to do that.

And so, I am once again in the banshee-free world of reality, on my way home to my wife and children in a large house in the country my father's money has made possible for me (the fruits, puzzlingly enough of his miserliness). It's not exactly suburbia with a white picket fence, but close enough. I have my little problems most days (did I remember to pick up more diapers? Do we need milk?), but they provide reassuring friction that anchors me to what is rather than to what was, the faint memory of other worlds I have lived in like momentary strange memories of Rwanda, or Munich, or for that matter high school— momentary shadows that fall on the surface of the water as the sun goes for an instant behind a cloud and then disappear in the full-lit languidity of the sunny summer day. Now I accept that the disparate worlds of life do not form part of a whole, save in a trivial sense. Instead all of us are the fragmentary bits of many novels begun and then laid aside, perhaps all returned to the shelves or the library in a once-a-month or once-a-semester housecleaning: who knows or cares if we finished them?

Birth or death?

For a time early in 2004 I wondered, would my father die before my second son was born, or the reverse? I felt as if I was evenly poised between birth and death, caught in the absolute center of my life. My son was born first, but it seemed a near thing. The day my father turned 90, he was in the hospital. Before that he lived without friends or acquaintances in his room in the assisted living facility. He spent his time doing what he has always spent his time doing, thinking of ways to avoid spending money. When finally the assisted living facility said he had gone beyond their capabilities and had to stay in the nursing home, he was furious—largely, I think, because it cost more.

After a bout in the first assisted living facility, he'd announced he felt the "sap of life" reviving and wanted a house. My mother, who at that point still did things for him, though they had been divorced for thirty years, went out and found him a little house to rent, up the street in Fruitland, Maryland, from where we grew up. He lasted three days before giving up. I suppose it was the life force refusing to give up; is this sad or admirable?

The next phase was to change residence constantly. He still drove his ancient Cadillac, that he used as overflow storage. He'd give notice at one Assisted Living Facility, have them put his few things in boxes in the trunk, and drive it to a new Assisted Living Facility he'd arranged to enter. Invariably he'd pronounce himself delighted, have three or four good months, and become disaffected once again. Once more, in this new place as in the one before it, the staff didn't come, they weren't doing what they were supposed to, he was leaving. I'd call and air his complaints; they'd explain patiently that nurses had three minutes to answer the buzzer and the time it had actually taken was entered in a log; looking at the log they saw no time over two minutes, and my father had never entered a complaint. He claimed they neglected him; they claimed they didn't. He moved to Annapolis, then to Crisfield, near where he grew up, then to Salisbury, then away, then back to Salisbury. At one point he even tried to buy a small house in a retirement community that presupposed much more independence than he actually could exercise. The developer, perplexed, called me for advice: I told him that frankly, my father wasn't up to it.

All these people telling him "no" simply infuriated him. Even from a wheelchair, which was the next step, he expected to be obeyed. He had me come to Salisbury, then drive him to Washington (total, four hours so far, in order to avoid the hospital across the street): Walter Reed Army Hospital was going to fix his hernia, and that was that. (He'd refused to buy the health insurance that would have allowed the civilian hospital to fix it for free: the Army was going to take care of him, he announced.) The doctors demurred: he was too old, it wasn't operable. On the way home he urinated all over my car seat. It stank (it turned out he had a urinary tract infection, for which he was subsequently treated). He didn't apologize. In fact, he didn't acknowledge it had happened. And as I dragged this sack of potatoes that was my father out of the front seat of my car, exhausted after the day's driving (by now up to eight hours) and stinking of his own urine, anger—largely at myself that I had gone along with his cockamamie plan to take him hundreds of miles out of my way so the Army could pay for an operation he alone insisted he needed—overcame pity. I swore to myself that never again would I do as he asked if I didn't think it was a good idea. He was wrong for most of my childhood; why should I think he was right now?

Bruises

I couldn't have known at the time that my next visit to a hospital would be not for my father, but for my son Owen. On the days when I wasn't a house-husband, I took him to day care. Meg's feelings of guilt at having to leave her baby with another woman were assuaged to a degree by the fact that "Miss Cindy," an officer's wife, was the most over-qualified day-care provider imaginable—a pediatric nurse, in fact, who spent her working life in Neo-natal Intensive Care, and at this point looked after her own two-year-old daughter.

One day when I picked Owen up from Miss Cindy, I noted bruises on his face, around his eyes like a raccoon, on his forehead and cheeks. I pointed them out to Miss Cindy, who had not noticed them: the light was dim in her apartment, and Owen had just awoken from a nap. She was puzzled, and concerned.

Meg was concerned too, and insisted on my taking Owen the next morning to the pediatrician. I emphasized to the doctor that there was almost no possibility that Owen had been shaken or mishandled by Miss Cindy, in whom we had complete trust. Nonetheless the pediatrician recommended we take him to Johns Hopkins Hospital to be checked over: the bruises were not normal. He would arrange the tests. Better to be safe than sorry, though of course it would turn out to be nothing. As the pediatrician said, "He looks so healthy!"

The next day was Friday; we were planning on going to New York that evening. Bright and early, however, we drove to Baltimore to get it out of the way. Hours went by as a string of women at increasing levels of importance and competence attempted to draw Owen's blood. The first gave up, the second, a certified phlebotomist, got a small amount of blood which turned out to be insufficient. By the time we were at the pediatric nurse level, they were sticking needles in his scalp. Then he was given a noxious anesthetic cocktail that took time to work. Limp and clad only in a diaper, he was strapped to a board and fed first through a CAT scan. We changed rooms and nurses, and his board was placed and re-placed under an X-ray machine in a darkened room.

It seemed so unnecessary to me, fuming at the incredibly sophisticated level of technology coupled with what was clearly sheer human incompetence (we had been sent to Hopkins because "they were so good at getting babies' blood!"). And all for something that surely would turn out to be nothing. After all, we had a trip to New York to make. Finally, however, it was mid-afternoon and the tests were done; we picked up Alexandra on the way out of town, returned home to regroup, and hit the road, taking the rural more scenic route across the upper Eastern Shore.

In the middle of the darkened corn fields, shrouded in snowless winter, the cell phone rang. Meg answered it. It was the pediatrician, who had gotten the test results. As she listened, she began to cry. My heart skipped a beat, Alexandra was oblivious on her earphones in the back, her shoulders convulsing to the music, Meg's at what she was hearing.

"Okay," I heard her say. "Okay." Then she hung up and began openly to sob. All around us was darkness.

The test results had come back. Owen had no platelets and minimal white blood cells. The most likely reason was leukemia. We were to turn around immediately and go back to Hopkins, or continue at once to CHOP, Children's Hospital of Philadelphia. He was in danger of "spontaneous bleeding."

We were still closer to Hopkins, and we could drop Alexandra off at her mother's. I wheeled the car around and set off in the direction from which we had come. I had tried to call Martha to let her know we were bringing back Alexandra, but had been disconnected. She called back, and I told her the situation. "Oh my God" was all she could say.

In a few minutes I got Alexandra's attention by tapping on her leg, told her we were going to have to have the weekend in New York another time, that Owen might be sick, and that we were going back to Mommy's house. "Okay," she said, putting her headphones back on.

An hour later, for the first time ever—buffered by my wife and (so it seemed) mortally ill child—I entered the kitchen of Martha's house. Her husband was away on business. She was solicitude and sympathy personified, and gave us leftovers to eat.

"This is the first time I've ever seen you and Mommy in the same room," Alexandra informed me.

Meg nursed Owen in Martha's living room and wept.

We then set out again for Baltimore, where, in the pediatric Emergency Room of Johns Hopkins Hospital, they were waiting for us. In hospitals there is no night or day, certainly not in an E R. The hallways were stark with fluorescent light, the walls some sort of white plasterboard. They were doing construction on part of it, from which hung plastic sheets, and part of the carpet had been removed. In a waiting room sat a policeman with a small boy.

Owen was whisked away to a room with a huge refrigerator-sized germ sucker, set up for a bubble boy such as they took him to be who could tolerate none of the normal background infection that human habitats are heir to. Yet puzzlingly, a few minutes later, two women came and creakingly wheeled away the germ sucker. "It turns out it's just his platelets that are low," one said in explanation. A few minutes later they wheeled it back. The same woman smiled, again apologetically. "The white blood count is low too," one nurse said. Even in illness there is comedy.

Even though it was the middle of the night, soon we had had a visit from the Pediatric Oncology professor, who had stayed around rather than going home to her family because she knew if she didn't she'd have to come back anyway, then from the ER doctor, and from countless nurses and residents. Two of the nurses set about once again, for what seemed the tenth time that day, drawing blood. Soon they were joined by a pediatrician, who turned out the lights of the room and shone a tiny flashlight on Owen's translucent skin in search of a vein. Finally she gave up on the arms ("all the veins are collapsed," she said) and, after taping his foot in flexed position to a board, ran a tube into his instep. At 6 a.m. they would begin taking bone samples. Leukemia was still the probable diagnosis.

There was talk of moving us upstairs to a room that was countermanded a few minutes later. By now it was 2:30 a.m. Blood work to confirm the first diagnosis came back. There were no readings at all for either platelets or white blood cells. The pediatrician explained, "Usually that means that they're so low they have to re-test." I felt the horror of the fluorescent lights, artificial brightness under which so much pain was happening, pain for a creature you love but can't protect. Owen himself seemed lost in a kind of merciful oblivion to the tubes invading his tiny body as he nursed and, fitfully, slept. I thought that this would be the first of many days and nights spent watching him be bled or treated. This too, I thought, is the way people sicken, and die—at every death bed is the texture of the sheet, the feel of one's tongue in one's mouth, a bit of dust in the corner. And the artificial lights. For us there was too the comedy of the germ sucking refrigerator and the trivial reality of the pediatrician's seal ring, which had turned around on her finger.

By now Meg, ever efficient and surely into planning mode to beat back panic, had figured out how we would cope and was telling me about it in the darkened, suddenly quiet room containing the three of us: she would quit her job, she said, so she could be with him during the treatment. We might move closer to the hospital. Our lives would be devoted to his cure.

What kind of strange dream had I been dreaming, I wondered, when I had thought I could start again, awakening into a new dawn of wife and children? I had lived through a horrible marriage that made me hate the woman I had once loved more dearly than any other; I had wanted to be the best father in the world to her children yet had listened to one of these children spew horror in various psychiatric hospitals; I been beaten up by a lawyer in pursuit of what I knew was the right thing for my daughter, who turned out to be learning-disabled and unable to access, save with great difficult, the feelings of others. This was my dream, and I was condemned to dream it to the end.

Every time a new nurse came in, I had to move my chair and hover awkwardly in the corner. As if taking charge of something small because I had no control over the larger things, I announced that I was going home, a forty minute drive, to sleep a few hours. Meg agreed I should. "Somebody has to," she said. I would be back before the tests at 6, bone marrow samples. More probes and sharp things were going to be stuck into the tiny body of my infant son.

I drove through the shabby, deserted streets of East Baltimore for the fourth time that day, my landmark for the right turn from Broadway a now-deserted porn-movie theater. XXX its marquee said each time in the streetlights, above an overflowing trash can on the corner. I arrived home and fell on the bed, fully clothed.

I must have slept fitfully for a few minutes before the phone rang. It was Meg. "It's good news," she said.

"What?" I said, struggling to come to the surface.

"The second blood tests came back," she said, "and then third ones. He's normal. He's okay."

"He's okay?" I repeated stupidly.

"The first test was an error," she said.

At least I was now wide awake. I was furious. "An error? Fuck," I said.

"You don't have to come get us," she said. "They said we could stay here till morning."

"Give me a break," I said. Did she really think I would simply turn over and go back to sleep?

I drove to Baltimore again. At least its streets were still deserted. By now it was close to 5. I parked in the garage yet again, stomped past the same hospital guards, who recognized me, down the almost deserted hallway, and into the ER, reining myself in briefly before I entered.

The hallways were no less brilliantly and garishly lit than before. But at one end of the corridor a party seemed in progress which, as I neared, abruptly transformed into a version of the final scene of Fellini's autobiographical artist-in-crisis movie *8 ½*, a gathering of all the actors we have met playing various roles throughout the movie. Owen, released from his coils of tubes and the tape that had covered his skin, rode pink-cheeked and laughing on the shoulders of a tall male nurse; around him all the various doctors and nurses we had seen in the course of the night talked excitedly, laughing and smiling. The pediatrician told us later that the ER staff had never had a child with this bad an initial prognosis be so thoroughly cleared of biological abnormality. Perhaps they were happy that at least one child, in the batch destined to be fed to Moloch, had been put aside, one given a reprieve.

By now I was at least outwardly in control, though inside I still seethed. How could they have done this to him, to us? They handed him over, somewhat reluctantly it seemed to me: with his absence the impromptu party was over, and they would have to go back to children who really were mortally ill. Because this one child was, inexplicably, spared, didn't mean they all were.

I retained the presence of mind to thank all the doctors and nurses profusely and then collected Meg from the same room I had left her in. Still, I was angry, though I couldn't have said why or at what. Shouldn't I be vowing to walk to Lourdes on my knees? And we passed through the guards, hugging our child like any happy little family. For the last time that day, I drove through the now not quite so deserted streets of East Baltimore, turning at the porn theater, which was unchanged and oblivious to our little drama, its marquee still saying XXX though somewhat more wanly in the hint of dawn opening up before us, and then home again, where we fell into bed.

When we awoke, it was 8 o'clock, the sun streaming in our window and onto the wrinkled bedclothes. Meg called the few people she had not called in the night (both mothers had been on the earlier list), and then we turned to each other and said at practically the same time, "Let's go to New York!" It seemed important to go through with our initial plan. And so we did, collecting Alexandra from Martha who seemed as delighted and relieved as we ourselves were that Owen had been given a stay of execution. The silver lining was perhaps that Martha's reaction during this crisis subsequently allowed us to have a relationship without quite so deep a chill, though from her perspective the chill was all on my side: she didn't understand what she had done, either during our marriage or its dissolution. And I gave up thinking she ever would.

And so we resumed our happy lives of a new family with plans for expansion, going back to noting Owen's development—crawling, his first tooth, delighting in his constant smiles, with the big sister, Alexandra, holding the little brother, both with blue eyes and strawberry-blonde hair: a family looking optimistically toward the future, horrors fading once again back into their coffin from which they had threatened to arise into day. And beyond that, the next little boy.

But that night in the hospital, when it seemed our apparently so healthy little boy was mortally ill and that we would spend the rest of our lives watching him suffer, the tragic sense of life had had the upper hand. It was at any rate a path that I could visualize, no less real than any other.

And then the celestial traffic policeman reconsidered, saying yes, this path exists, yes you could well be directed to take it. But not now, not today. Go back home with your wife and laughing child. Believe that things turn out all right in the end. Because sometimes they do.

Author Biography

Bruce Fleming won an O. Henry Award for his first published story, "The Autobiography of Gertrude Stein" (1991) and in 2005, the Antioch Review Award for Distinguished Prose, a career award. His experimental novel *Twilley* (1997) was compared by critics to works by Henry James, T.S. Eliot, Proust, Thoreau, and David Lynch. He has published a book of dance essays, *Sex, Art and Audience* (2000), many scholarly and theoretical books, and articles and essays in literary quarterlies and publications such as the *Village Voice*, *The Washington Post*, and *The Nation*. His most recent books include *Life, Death and Literature at the U.S. Naval Academy* (2005), *Why Liberals and Conservatives Clash* (2006) and *The New Tractatus* (2007). He is an English professor at the U.S. Naval Academy, Annapolis.